AQA

Physics for GCSE Combined Science: Trilogy

Foundation Workbook

Helen Reynolds
Editor: Lawrie Ryan

T0346843

OXFORD
UNIVERSITY PRESS

Great Clarendon Street, Oxford, OX2 6DP, United Kingdom

Oxford University Press is a department of the University of Oxford.
It furthers the University's objective of excellence in research,
scholarship, and education by publishing worldwide. Oxford is a
registered trade mark of Oxford University Press in the UK and in
certain other countries

British Library Cataloguing in Publication Data
Data available

978 0 19 835936 4

10 9 8

Paper used in the production of this book is a natural, recyclable
product made from wood grown in sustainable forests.
The manufacturing process conforms to the environmental regulations
of the country of origin.

Printed in Great Britain by CPI Group (UK) Ltd., Croydon CR0 4YY

Cover: Johnér / Offset

p9: macrovector/shutterstock; **p82**: wang song/shutterstock;

All artwork by Q2A media

Contents

Any topics omitted from your workbook and from this contents page are Higher tier.

4 Waves and electromagnetism

Chapter P11 Wave properties

Chapter P12 Electromagnetic waves

Chapter P13 Electromagnetism

Introduction

Practice activities – Lots of varied questions, increasing in difficulty, to build your confidence and help you progress through the course

What you need to remember – Each topic from your GCSE Student Book is covered, and includes a summary of the key content you need to know

Hints – Handy hints to give you extra guidance on how to answer more complex questions

Checklists – Use the checklists to ensure you have covered the required learning outcomes and are ready to move on to the next chapter

Practice questions – Practice questions appear at the end of each chapter, to test your knowledge. They include a mix of short and long-answer question types, as well as practical-focused questions so you can practise the key skills required for your examinations. All answers are in the Workbook, allowing for instant feedback and self-assessment

P1.1 Changes in energy stores

A There are different types of energy store. A store is a way of keeping track of energy.

Draw a line to match each type of store to an example of the store.

Type of store	Example
energy in a chemical store	a hot cup of coffee
energy in a kinetic store	food, fuels, and chemicals in batteries
energy in a gravitational potential store	a moving skateboarder
energy in an elastic potential store	a stretched catapult
energy in a thermal store	a climber at the top of Mount Everest

B Different processes transfer energy between stores.

Circle the correct **bold** words and phrases in the sentences below.

When you turn on a phone charger, you are transferring energy by **an electric current/heating** to the chemical energy store of the battery.

During a bungee jump, **a force/heating** transfers energy to an elastic store.

When you cool down after a PE lesson, energy is transferred by **a force/heating**, and by **an electric current/waves**.

C If you drop a tennis ball it bounces, but if you drop your keys they do not bounce.

Tick the boxes to describe the energy stores and transfers. Some are true for **both** the tennis ball and the keys.

Description of energy store/transfer	✓ if true for tennis ball	✓ if true for keys
energy in the gravitational potential energy store at the start		
energy transferred by forces		
energy transferred by heating/sound		
energy in the gravitational potential energy store at the end		
energy in the thermal energy store at the end		

What you need to remember

An energy _____ is a way of keeping track of energy.

You can transfer energy by _____, by _____, by _____, and by _____ .

When an object falls, the energy in its _____ _____ energy store decreases, and the energy in its _____ energy store increases.

When an object hits the ground but does not bounce, the energy in its _____ energy store decreases. Energy is transferred to the _____ by sound waves and by _____ .

P1.2 Conservation of energy

A Write down the principle of conservation of energy.

_____

_____

_____

B A system is an object or a group of objects.

Choose the correct statement about closed systems. Circle the letter of the correct statement.

W There is no energy transfer into a closed system.

X Energy can be transferred into the system as long as the temperature stays the same.

Y There is no energy transfer in or out of a closed system.

Z In a closed system the objects cannot move.

C An astronaut is on the Moon, where there is no air. He is holding a pendulum that is swinging.

Tick the correct statement about the energy transfers.

Statement	✓ if correct
The pendulum is not a closed system because energy is transferred to the surroundings.	
The maximum kinetic energy is equal to the maximum gravitational potential energy.	
As the pendulum swings the air gets a bit hotter.	
If there was friction the swinging pendulum would be a closed system.	

D What would happen if everyday situations became closed systems?

Circle the correct **bold** words and phrases in the sentences below.

If a bouncing ball was a closed system then the ball would reach **a lower/the same** height at each bounce.

If a child on a swing was a closed system you **would/would not** need to push them again after the first push.

If a bungee jumper was a closed system the person **would/would not** come to a stop.

What you need to remember

Energy cannot be _____ or _____ . This is the principle of _____ of energy, which applies to _____ energy changes.

An isolated system is called a _____ system. There are no _____ transfers into or out of the system.

If there are transfers within the system then the total energy does not _____ .

P1.3 Energy and work

A Circle the correct **bold** words and phrases to make the correct scientific definition of **work**.

You do work when you use a **force/mass** to move an object **a certain distance/at a certain speed**.

B You do work in lots of situations every day.

Tick the situations that involve doing mechanical work.

Situation	✓ if it involves doing work
lying in bed	
cycling to school	
lifting your bag into your locker	
using a power pack to light a bulb	

C Complete the table by calculating the work done by each force.

Remember to use standard units of metres and newtons, and to write down the unit of work.

Force	Distance	Work done
10 N	2 m	
30 N	10 cm	
25 kN	5 m	
20 kN	50 mm	

D A father pushing a buggy does work against friction. He pushes the buggy 10 m using a force of 15 N.

Complete the calculation to find the work done by the father.

work done (J) = force (N) × distance (m)

= _____ N × _____ m

= _____ J

15 N

What you need to remember

'Work' in science is about using a _____ to move an object. Work is a way of _____ energy between energy stores.

You can calculate work using this equation, with the units in the brackets:

work done (_____) = _____ (_____) × _____ (_____)

[You need to remember this equation.]

When an object moves through the air it does work against _____ , or when you slide it across the floor it does work against _____ .

These processes _____ the surroundings.

P1.4 Gravitational potential energy stores

A How does **gravitational potential energy** increase or decrease in different situations?

Draw a line to match each situation to the correct statement about gravitational potential energy.

Situation

You go up in a lift.

You walk downstairs.

You run 100 m on a flat track.

Statement

The energy in your gravitational potential energy store stays the same.

The energy in your gravitational potential energy store increases.

The energy in your gravitational potential energy store decreases.

B When you lift an object in a gravitational field, there is a change in the gravitational potential energy store of the object.

Calculate the change in the gravitational potential energy store for the objects in the table. Remember to use standard units of newtons and metres, and to write down the unit of gravitational potential energy.

Mass of object	Gravitational field strength in N/kg	Change in height	Change in gravitational potential energy store
1 kg	10	2 m	
1 kg	1.6	10 cm	
250 g	27	5 m	
20 g	10	50 mm	

C There is a change in the gravitational potential energy store when you lift a suitcase into a car. The weight of the suitcase is 100 N.

Complete the calculation to find the change in the gravitational potential energy store.

change in gravitational potential energy = weight (N) × change in height (m)

= _____ N × _____ m

= _____ J

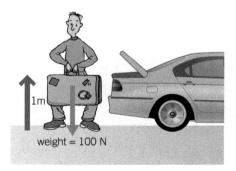

1m

weight = 100 N

What you need to remember

The gravitational potential energy of an object _____ when it is lifted up and _____ when it is moved down.

You do _____ when you lift something up to overcome the gravitational _____ . The gravitational field strength on the Moon is _____ than it is on the Earth, so it is _____ to lift an object up on the Moon than on the Earth.

You can calculate the change in the gravitational potential energy store using this equation, with units in the brackets:

change in gravitational potential energy store (_____) = _____ (_____) × _____ field _____ (_____) × change of _____ (_____)

[You need to remember this equation.]

P1.5 Kinetic energy and elastic energy stores

A An object that is moving has **kinetic energy**.

Circle the quantities that kinetic energy depends on.

mass   distance travelled   power   speed   force

B Describe what is meant by **elastic potential energy**.

_____

_____

_____

C A student uses light gates to find the speed of a ball just before it hits the ground. She finds that the speed is 10 m/s. The mass of the ball is 50 g. There are 1000 g in 1 kg.

Convert the mass to kilograms and complete the calculation to find the kinetic energy of the ball.

kinetic energy (J) = 0.5 × mass (kg) × (speed (m/s))²

$= 0.5 \times$ _____ (kg) × (_____ (m/s))²

$=$ _____ J

HINT Don't forget to square the speed in this calculation.

D In activity **C** the ball bounces. There is a point at which all the energy in the kinetic store of the ball is transferred to an elastic store.

Write down what the ball is doing at this point.

_____

_____

E Which spring below has the most elastic potential energy?

Circle the correct letter.

X a spring of spring constant 50 N/m stretched by 0.1 m

Y a spring of spring constant 100 N/m stretched by 0.2 m

Z a spring of spring constant 50 N/m stretched by 0.2 m

HINT Try to work out the springs with the least and the most energy without using the equation.

What you need to remember

The kinetic energy of an object depends on its _____ and its _____ .

You can calculate kinetic energy using this equation, with units in the brackets:

kinetic energy = 0.5 × _____ (_____) × (_____ (_____))²

[You need to remember this equation.]

When you stretch or compress an object, you do _____ and transfer energy to an _____ store.

[You can use this equation on the Physics equation sheet to calculate the change in elastic potential energy:

elastic potential energy = 0.5 × spring constant (N/kg) × (extension (m))²]

P1.6 Energy dissipation

A Draw a line to match each word or phrase to its correct definition.

useful energy	energy that is transferred by a pathway that we do not want
wasted energy	the process of energy spreading out so it is not useful
dissipation	energy that is transferred by a pathway that we want

B On a car journey there are lots of energy transfers.

Tick the correct column to show if each energy transfer is useful or wasted.

Energy that is transferred to a ...	✓ if it is useful energy output	✓ if it is wasted energy output
kinetic store when the car accelerates		
thermal store of the surroundings due to friction between the gears		
thermal store of the brakes and surroundings due to friction when slowing down		
thermal store of the surroundings due to light from the headlights		

C For each of the activities below, fill in the column with **one** pathway that dissipates energy. For example, energy is dissipated due to heating by particles (air resistance, sound) when a plane moves through the air.

Write down both the pathway and the physical process.

Activity	Pathway that dissipates energy
riding a bicycle	
using an electric drill	
using an electric oven	

What you need to remember

Useful energy is energy transferred in a pathway that we _____ .

In any device or process energy spreads out, which we call _____ .

Energy that is not useful is _____ . This energy is eventually transferred to the

_____ , which become _____ .

P1.7 Energy and efficiency

A How efficient can a device be?

Circle the maximum efficiency possible below.

| 0.1% | 1% | 10% | 100% | 1000% |

B Tick to show if each statement about efficiency is true or false.

Statement	✓ if true	✓ if false
A more efficient device wastes more energy than a less efficient one.		
A less efficient device wastes more energy than an efficient one.		
If you had a less efficient device, you would need more input energy to get the same output energy.		

C You can use oil to lubricate surfaces that are in contact in a machine.

Circle the correct **bold** words in the sentences below.

Lubricating the chain of your bicycle is a **bad/good** idea because it **decreases/increases** friction, and **decreases/increases** the energy wasted. Lubricating the surface of your brake blocks is a **bad/good** idea because it **decreases/increases** friction, which makes it **easier/harder** to stop.

When you come to a stop on your bicycle the force of friction transfers energy to the **gravitational/thermal** store of the surroundings.

D A motor has an input energy transfer of 1000 J and a useful output energy transfer of 400 J.

Complete the calculation of **efficiency**.

$$efficiency = \frac{useful\ energy\ transfer\ (J)}{total\ input\ energy\ transfer\ (J)}$$

$$= \frac{\underline{\hspace{2cm}}\ J}{\underline{\hspace{2cm}}\ J}$$

$$= \underline{\hspace{2cm}}$$

What you need to remember

You can calculate efficiency using this equation, with units in the brackets:

$$efficiency = \frac{\underline{\hspace{2cm}}\ output\ energy\ transfer\ (\underline{\hspace{1cm}})}{\underline{\hspace{2cm}}\ input\ energy\ transfer\ (\underline{\hspace{1cm}})}$$

[*You need to remember this equation.*]

No device can be more than _____ % efficient, because this would mean that energy has been

_____ .

Machines waste energy because of _____ between moving parts, by _____ the air when they are moving, and by getting _____ when a current flows. You can reduce the amount of wasted energy by _____ the surfaces between moving parts.

P1.8 Electrical appliances

A We use lots of different types of energy source in our homes.

Select words from the list below to complete the sentences. You can use the words once, more than once, or not at all.

wood   **coal**   **electricity**   **gas**

a   You usually cook pizza using _____ or _____ .

b   You use _____ or _____ in your central heating.

c   You use _____ when you watch television.

B You can use an electric kettle or an oven to heat water. In each case, energy is transferred to the thermal store of the water.

a   Which appliance would you choose to heat water, a kettle or an oven? _____

b   Write down **one** reason for your answer.

_____

_____

_____

C Here are some data about different types of light bulb. The bulbs appear equally bright.

Light bulb	Energy supplied to light bulb in 1 minute
X	700 J
Y	2500 J

a   Circle in blue the letter of the light bulb that is more efficient.

b   Circle in red the letter of the light bulb that wastes more energy.

c   Explain your answer to **b**.

_____

_____

_____

What you need to remember

Most of the energy that people use in their homes is supplied by gas, _____ , or electricity.

_____ is a clean and efficient way of transferring energy to many of the appliances that you use every day. You use electrical appliances for _____ (e.g., in an oven), _____ (e.g., a low-energy lamp), moving objects (e.g., the turntable in a _____ oven), and creating sound and images.

More efficient electrical appliances waste _____ energy than less-efficient electrical devices.

P1.9 Energy and power

A Draw lines to link the correct words from each column to make **one** sentence that defines **power**.

| time | | divided by | | the time. |

Power is the

| energy transferred | | multiplied by | | the energy transferred. |

B Tick to show if each statement about power is true or false.

Statement	✓ if true	✓ if false
Powerful devices are always more efficient than less powerful devices.		
A less powerful device transfers more useful energy per second than a more powerful one.		
You would need to run a less powerful device for longer to get the same energy transfer as a more powerful device.		

C A lift carries you to the top floor of a building, transferring 100 000 J of energy in 20 s.

a Complete the calculation to find the useful power output of the lift.

$$\text{power (W)} = \frac{\text{energy (J)}}{\text{time (s)}}$$

$$= \frac{\rule{2cm}{0.4pt} \text{ J}}{\rule{2cm}{0.4pt} \text{ s}}$$

$$= \rule{2cm}{0.4pt} \text{ W}$$

b The total power input to the lift is 20 kW.

Complete the calculation to find the percentage efficiency of the lift.

HINT Remember to convert power to watts.

$$\text{efficiency} = \frac{\text{useful power out}}{\text{total power in}} \times 100\%$$

$$= \frac{\rule{2cm}{0.4pt} \text{ W}}{\rule{2cm}{0.4pt} \text{ W}} \times 100\%$$

$$= \rule{2cm}{0.4pt} \%$$

c Complete the calculation to find the wasted power.

$$\text{wasted power} = \text{total power input (W)} - \text{useful power output (W)}$$

$$= \rule{2cm}{0.4pt} \text{ W} - \rule{2cm}{0.4pt} \text{ W}$$

$$= \rule{2cm}{0.4pt} \text{ W}$$

What you need to remember

Power is the _____ of energy transfer.

You can calculate power using this equation, with units in the brackets:

$$\text{power} = \frac{\rule{2cm}{0.4pt} (\rule{1cm}{0.4pt})}{\rule{2cm}{0.4pt} (\rule{1cm}{0.4pt})}$$ **[You need to remember this equation.]**

You can calculate efficiency as a percentage using this equation, with units in the brackets:

$$\text{percentage efficiency} = \frac{\rule{2cm}{0.4pt} \text{ power out } (\rule{1cm}{0.4pt}) \times 100\%}{\rule{2cm}{0.4pt} \text{ power in } (\rule{1cm}{0.4pt})}$$ **[You need to remember this equation.]**

You can calculate the power that is wasted using this equation:

power wasted = _____ power in − _____ power out

P1 Practice questions

01 Sort the words below into types of energy store and processes that transfer energy. Write the words in the correct column of **Table 1**. [2 marks]

**thermal   conduction   electric current
elastic potential   kinetic   gravitational
radiation   forces   chemical**

Table 1

Type of energy store	Type of transfer pathway

02 You drop a ball and it bounces.
Circle the correct **bold** words in the sentences below. [2 marks]

When the ball stops briefly when it hits the floor there is energy in the **elastic/kinetic** store of the ball. It was transferred to this store by **a force/heating**.

03 Draw a line to match each quantity to its definition. [2 marks]

Quantity	Definition
work done	a ratio or percentage that tells you how good a device is at transferring energy
power	the energy transferred when a force moves through a distance
efficiency	the rate of energy transfer

04 A government scientist was assessing the efficiency of kettles. **Table 2** shows data from her experiment.

Table 2

Kettle	Energy required to boil water in J	Energy supplied to kettle in J
A	300 000	400 000
B	300 000	450 000

04.1 Write down **one** variable that the scientist would have kept the same in this experiment. [1 mark]

04.2 Calculate the efficiency of kettle **A** as a percentage. [3 marks]

> **HINT** Find the ratio of the useful energy to the total energy input.

04.3 Without doing a calculation, write down if kettle **B** is more or less efficient than kettle **A**. [1 mark]

04.4 Suggest **one** reason for using electricity rather than solid fuel to heat water. [1 mark]

04.5 Suggest **one** process that wastes energy when the kettle is working. [1 mark]

> **HINT** Think about how energy is transferred to the surroundings.

05 About 100 years ago there was an event in the Olympic Games called the 'standing high jump'. An athlete stood still, then jumped vertically. The world record is 1.9 m.

05.1 If the mass of the athlete is 50 kg, and gravitational field strength is 10 N/kg, show that the energy transferred to the gravitational potential energy store when he jumped is about 1000 J. [3 marks]

> **HINT** Use $E_g = m \times g \times h$

05.2 The athlete in **05.1** is travelling at 6 m/s just before he lands again. Show that his kinetic energy is 900 J. [3 marks]

> **HINT** Use $E_k = 0.5 \times m \times v^2$

05.3 Suggest where the 'missing energy' has gone. [1 mark]

05.4 The athlete bends his knees when he jumps and lands. Suggest which energy store is increased when he does this. [1 mark]

P1 Checklist

	Student Book	☺	☺	☹
I can describe the ways in which energy can be stored.	1.1			
I can describe how energy can be transferred.	1.1			
I can describe the energy transfers that happen when an object falls.	1.1			
I can describe the energy transfers that happen when a falling object hits the ground without bouncing back.	1.1			
I can describe what conservation of energy is.	1.2			
I can explain why conservation of energy is a very important idea.	1.2			
I can describe what a closed system is.	1.2			
I can describe energy transfers in a closed system.	1.2			
I can describe what work means in science.	1.3			
I can describe how work and energy are related.	1.3			
I can calculate the work done by a force.	1.3			
I can describe what happens to work that is done to overcome friction.	1.3			
I can describe what happens to the gravitational potential energy store of an object when it moves up or down.	1.4			
I can explain why an object moving up increases its gravitational potential energy store.	1.4			
I can explain why it is easier to lift an object on the Moon than on the Earth.	1.4			
I can calculate the change in gravitational potential energy of an object when it moves up or down.	1.4			
I can write down what the kinetic energy of an object depends on.	1.5			
I can calculate kinetic energy.	1.5			
I can describe what an elastic potential energy store is.	1.5			
I can calculate the amount of energy in an elastic potential energy store.	1.5			
I can describe what is meant by useful energy.	1.6			
I can describe what is meant by wasted energy.	1.6			
I can describe what eventually happens to wasted energy.	1.6			
I can describe if energy is still as useful after it is used.	1.6			
I can describe what is meant by efficiency.	1.7			
I can write down the maximum efficiency of any energy transfer.	1.7			
I can describe how machines waste energy.	1.7			
I can describe how energy is supplied to homes.	1.8			
I can explain why electrical appliances are useful.	1.8			
I can describe what most everyday electrical appliances are used for.	1.8			
I can explain how to choose an electrical appliance for a particular job.	1.8			
I can describe what is meant by power.	1.9			
I can calculate the power of an appliance.	1.9			
I can calculate the efficiency of an appliance in terms of power.	1.9			
I can calculate the power wasted by an appliance.	1.9			

P2.1 Energy transfer by conduction

A Some materials are good **conductors** and some materials are good **insulators**.

Sort the materials below by writing them in the correct column of the table.

copper   **wool**   **iron**   **aluminium**   **glass**   **fibreglass**

Good conductors	Good insulators

B What is thermal conductivity?

Circle the correct **bold** words below.

Thermal conductivity tells you the **amount/rate** of energy transfer through a material. A material with a **high/low** thermal conductivity conducts energy more quickly through it.

C The diagram shows an experiment to investigate conduction. The wax on rod **X** melts first, then the wax on rod **Z**, and finally the wax on rod **Y**.

Tick the boxes to show whether the statements are true or false.

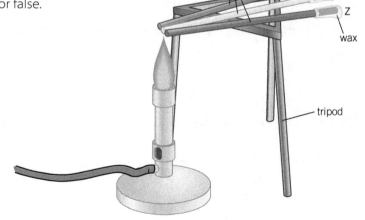

Statement	✓ if true	✓ if false
Rod **X** has the highest thermal conductivity.		
Rod **Y** has the lowest thermal conductivity.		
Rod **Y** could be made of metal.		
The wax on the rods would melt more slowly if they had a larger diameter.		

What you need to remember

The best conductors of energy are _____ . Materials such as wool and fibreglass, which are

_____ , are good insulators.

A material with a high thermal conductivity has a _____ rate of energy transfer through it.

The thicker a layer of insulating material, the _____ the rate of energy transfer through it.

P2.2 Specific heat capacity

A Write a sentence to describe what is meant by **specific heat capacity**.

_____

_____

_____

B Look at the amounts of energy in the table below.

Write the letters in order from the smallest to the largest amount of energy.

The specific heat capacity of aluminium is 900 J/kg °C, and the specific heat capacity of water is 4200 J/kg °C.

	Energy required to...
X	raise the temperature of 1 kg of aluminium by 10 °C
Y	raise the temperature of 1 kg of water by 20 °C
Z	raise the temperature of 1 kg of water by 10 °C

Correct order: _____

C A student puts 0.25 kg of water in an insulated beaker. She puts a heater in the beaker and switches it on. It raises the temperature of the water by 10 °C in 10 minutes.

Complete the calculation to find the change in thermal energy.

The specific heat capacity of water is 4200 J/kg °C.

change in thermal energy (J) = mass (kg) × specific heat capacity (J/kg °C) × change in temperature (°C)

= _____ kg × _____ J/kg °C × _____ °C

= _____ J

D Suggest what the student would notice if she used twice as much water in the experiment as in activity **C**.

_____

_____

What you need to remember

The specific heat capacity is the energy needed to change the temperature of _____ of a substance by _____ °C.

Using a heater with the same rate of energy transfer, a more massive piece of a substance will take _____ to heat up than a less massive piece of the same substance.

To find the specific heat capacity you need to measure the _____ using a joulemeter, the temperature difference using a _____, and the _____ using a digital balance.

[You can use this equation on the Physics equation sheet to calculate the change in thermal energy:

change in thermal energy (J) = mass (kg) × specific heat capacity (J/kg °C) × change in temperature (°C)]

P2.3 Heating and insulating buildings

A Here are some fuels and some energy transfer devices used for heating in people's homes.

Tick the boxes to show which fuels each type of device may use. Each device may use more than one fuel.

Fuel	✓ if it may be burned in a stove	✓ if it may be used in a central heating system	✓ if it may be burned on a fire
oil			
coal or wood			
gas			

B Describe what cavity wall insulation is.

_____

_____

_____

C Insulating a house can reduce the rate of energy transfer from it, saving money on energy bills.

Write an **R** next to the methods that would be good for reducing the rate of energy transfer from a house.

Methods

building a house using thick bricks

putting layers of fibreglass in the loft

using a material with a high thermal conductivity to insulate the house

using aluminium foil behind the radiators

D A family buys double glazing which costs £2000, and which saves £100 per year on their heating bills.

Circle the correct **payback time** in years.

2   20   200   2000   20 000   200 000

What you need to remember

People use heaters that run on electricity or _____ to heat their homes, or central heating that runs on _____ or gas. Solid fuel such as coal or _____ is often burned in stoves for heating.

People can reduce the energy transfer from the loft of a house using _____ _____ .

They can reduce the rate of energy transfer through windows using _____ _____ .

There are usually _____ layers of brick in the walls of a house, with a layer of _____ _____ insulation to reduce the rate of energy transfer. It also helps to use bricks on the outside that are _____ and have a _____ thermal conductivity.

P2 Practice questions

01 There are many different ways of reducing energy transfer from a house. Draw a line to match each type of insulation to the part of a house where it is used. [2 marks]

loft insulation	windows
thick bricks	roof
double glazing	walls

02 Here is a list of materials. Circle the ones that are good conductors. [2 marks]

iron   foam   wool   steel   copper   glass

03 A student puts equal masses of water at 70 °C into three different cans:

    A shiny metal can

    B shiny black can

    C matt black can.

She measures the temperature 10 minutes later.

03.1 Write the letter of the can with the lowest temperature. [1 mark]

_____

03.2 Write the type of radiation emitted by the cans. [1 mark]

_____

04 Tick the boxes in **Table 1** to show whether each of the following statements about thermal conductivity and specific heat capacity is true or false. [2 marks]

Table 1

	✓ if true	✓ if false
04.1		
04.2		
04.3		
04.4		

04.1 A material with a high thermal conductivity transfers energy at a low rate.

04.2 The specific heat capacity tells you the energy you need to transfer to a mass of substance to raise its temperature by 1 °C.

04.3 A material with a high specific heat capacity will heat up slowly.

04.4 The thermal conductivity of a material tells you about the rate of energy transfer through the material.

HINT If you know the units of quantities, this helps you work out what they mean.

05 **Figure 1** shows some equipment that you could use to measure the specific heat capacity of a substance.

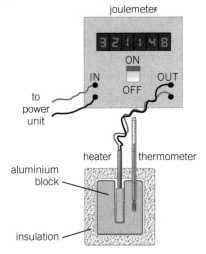

Figure 1

05.1 Fill in the gaps to describe what each piece of equipment in **Figure 1** is for.

    a You use the _____ to measure the energy transferred. [1 mark]

    b You use the _____ to measure the temperature rise. [1 mark]

05.2 A student makes the following measurements using an aluminium block.

temperature rise = 20 °C

mass of block = 1 kg

energy transferred = 45 J

Use these measurements to calculate the specific heat capacity of aluminium. [2 marks]

Use this equation:

specific heat capacity J/kg °C =

$$\frac{\text{energy (J)}}{\text{mass (kg)} \times \text{temperature change (°C)}}$$

_____

_____

_____

_____

_____

HINT Multiply the mass and temperature change first, and then divide the energy by this number.

P2 Checklist

	Student Book	☺	😐	☹
I can write down which materials make the best conductors.	2.1			
I can write down which materials make the best insulators.	2.1			
I can describe how the thermal conductivity of a material affects the rate of energy transfer through it by conduction.	2.1			
I can describe how the thickness of a layer of material affects the rate of energy transfer through it by conduction.	2.1			
I can describe what the specific heat capacity of a substance means.	2.1			
I can calculate the energy needed to change the temperature of an object.	2.2			
I can describe how the mass of a substance affects how quickly its temperature changes when you heat it.	2.2			
I can describe how to measure the specific heat capacity of a substance.	2.2			
I can describe how homes are heated.	2.2			
I can describe how you can reduce the rate of energy transfer from your home.	2.3			
I can describe what cavity wall insulation is.	2.3			

P3.1 Energy demands

A Energy resources are classified as **non-renewable** or **renewable.**

a Circle the resources below in red if they are non-renewable.

b Circle them in blue if they are renewable.

c Put a black box around three main resources that we use to meet our current energy demands.

coal   **gas**   **wind**   **oil**   **nuclear**   **solar**   **biofuels**

B Circle the correct **bold** words and phrases in these sentences, which are about biofuels.

A biofuel comes from **living or recently living/fossilised** material. One example of a biofuel is animal waste. This provides **methane/oxygen** which can be burnt in a small power station. Another example of a biofuel is **ethanol/petrol**, which can be used in cars and is produced from sugar cane.

Biofuels are **non-renewable/renewable** because you can always grow more. They are **carbon-neutral/harmful** because as plants grow, they absorb the carbon dioxide released when you burn the biofuel.

C Draw a line to match each sentence start to its correct ending to describe what happens in a nuclear power station.

In the core, radioactive material such as uranium in the **nuclear fuel** rods	drives a **generator** to produce electricity.
The hot coolant is pumped around a heat exchanger and	releases energy from each uranium **nucleus,** which heats a coolant.
The steam drives a **turbine**, which	fossil fuels.
Uranium releases more energy per kilogram than	heats water to produce steam.

What you need to remember

We meet most of our energy demands by burning _____, _____, and _____ .

These energy resources are non-renewable which means that they _____ _____ run out.

Renewable resources will _____ run out.

Renewable fuels from living or recently living material are called _____ . One example is a gas called _____, and another example is a liquid called _____ .

We use uranium or plutonium in a _____ power station. These fuels release much _____ energy per kilogram than fossil fuels.

P3.2 Energy from wind and water

A **Renewable energy** resources include the wind, waves, and tides.

Draw a line to match each device that harnesses a renewable energy source to its description.

Device	Description
wind turbine	a generator that floats on water
wave generator	a dam containing generators that traps water behind it
tidal barrage	a generator on top of a tall tower

B Tick to show whether each of the statements below is true.

Statement	✓ if true
Wind energy does not come from the Sun.	
Tidal power is more reliable than wave power.	
Wave power and tidal power both rely on moving water.	
There are no disadvantages to wind power.	
Wave generators can damage the habitats of wildlife.	

C One of the first hydroelectric power stations was at Niagara Falls in the USA.

Describe what happens in a hydroelectric power station.

_____

_____

_____

What you need to remember

A wind _____ is an electricity generator on top of a tall tower.

A _____ generator is used to generate electricity from wave power.

Water stored in lakes or reservoirs can run downhill, flowing through _____ that turn generators. This is called _____ power.

In a _____ power station, water at high tide is trapped behind a barrage, then released to turn a generator.

Wind and wave power can be unreliable, and renewable resources can damage the _____ .

A Describe the difference between a solar heating panel and a solar cell panel.

_____

_____

_____

B Solar panels have advantages and disadvantages.

In the table below, write **A** if the statement refers to an advantage of solar panels,
D if it refers to a disadvantage, or **N** if it is neither an advantage nor a disadvantage.

Statement	A, D, or N?
Solar cells convert less than 10% of solar radiation into electricity.	
Solar panels only work on sunny days.	
You can generate electricity in remote places with solar cells.	
Solar cells are very expensive to buy.	
You do not need to be connected to a power station to use solar cells.	
Solar cells can be connected together to make solar cell panels.	
You need lots of solar cell panels to generate enough electricity to be useful.	

C **Geothermal** power stations are often built in volcanic areas.

Here are some stages in a description of how a geothermal power station works. Sort them into the correct order.

Write the letters in order below.

P The steam comes back up to a power station on the surface.

Q Radioactive substances deep within the Earth release energy.

R Water pumped down into the Earth is heated by the rocks and converted into steam.

S This heats the rocks deep in the Earth.

T Here the steam drives a turbine, which drives a generator to produce electricity.

Correct order: _____

What you need to remember

We use solar cells to _____ electricity. We use solar heating panels to _____ water directly.

Deep in the Earth, energy is released by _____ substances. This heats _____ that is

pumped deep down into the rocks. The water turns to _____, which drives _____ at the

Earth's surface to generate electricity.

P3.4 Energy and the environment

A Burning fossil fuels and using radioactive materials to generate electricity can cause problems.

Draw lines to link the boxes in each column to make **three** sentences about problems and possible solutions.

	produces carbon dioxide (a **greenhouse gas**),	which needs to be stored safely for centuries.
Burning fossil fuels		
	produces radioactive waste,	which can be removed from the atmosphere with **carbon capture and storage.**
Using nuclear fuels		
	produces sulfur dioxide,	which must be removed from the atmosphere so it does not cause **acid rain.**

B The table lists some disadvantages of renewable energy sources.

Tick the correct columns to show which renewable resources each disadvantage applies to. You may need to tick several columns for each disadvantage.

Disadvantage	Wind?	Tidal?	Hydro?	Solar?
Can cause noise pollution.				
Can affect river estuaries and the habitats of plants and animals there.				
Depends on the weather to work.				
Involves large reservoirs of water, which can affect the habitats of plants and animals.				
Needs large areas of land to produce enough energy from these panels.				
Not always available on demand.				

C Write down **one** major advantage of nuclear power over using fossil fuels that is not to do with waste gases.

_____

_____

_____

What you need to remember

Burning fossil fuels releases _____ gases, which could cause global _____ .

Nuclear fuels produce _____ waste.

Renewable energy resources _____ _____ produce harmful waste products, and they can be used in _____ places. They can take up a large area and disturb the habitats of _____ and _____ .

P3.5 Big energy issues

A There are problems with using resources for electricity generation.

Draw a line to match each problem to a solution.

Problem

global warming

acid rain

contamination from radioactive waste

Solution

find a secure place to store waste

carbon capture and storage

remove sulfur from fuel

B Circle the correct **bold** words and phrases in these sentences to describe the options for meeting future energy demands.

Our demand for energy is **decreasing/increasing**. Nuclear power stations are **cheap/expensive** to build, run, and **decommission/demolish**. Renewables are **cheap/expensive** to install, but **cheap/expensive** to run. We will need a **range of resources/single solution** to meet our future energy needs.

C Look at the graph showing the demand for electricity during a typical day.

a Suggest the times between which you:

i could store excess energy

_____

ii would need to release excess energy.

_____

b Suggest how excess energy is stored.

_____

_____

_____

_____

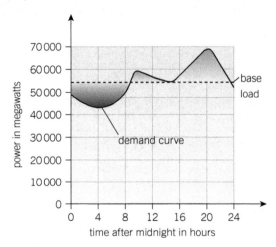

What you need to remember

The demand for electricity varies over the day, and during the year. You can meet this demand with _____ fired power stations and _____ storage. Nuclear power stations are _____ to build, run, and _____ (dismantle when you no longer need them).

The carbon dioxide produced by burning fuels can be removed from the atmosphere in a process called _____, but this is very expensive. Renewable resources are _____ to run but _____ to install. We are going to need a range of resources to meet future demand for energy.

P3 Practice questions

01 Generating electricity can use a variety of different fuels.

01.1 Circle the resources below that are fuels. [2 marks]

coal   uranium   wind   oil   gas   waves

01.2 Write down **three** main fuels from those that you have circled that we use today. [1 mark]

_____

02 Sort the statements into the correct order to explain how we generate electricity in a nuclear power station. Write the letters in order below. [4 marks]

   A   The steam drives turbines.

   B   The uranium nuclei split, which releases energy.

   C   The turbines turn generators to produce electricity.

   D   A coolant absorbs the energy and gets hot.

   E   The hot coolant heats water to produce steam.

   Correct order: _____

03 The Sun is used as an energy resource in a variety of ways. Circle the correct **bold** words and phrases in the sentences below.

03.1 The Sun can heat water in a **solar cell/ solar heating panel**. [1 mark]

03.2 You can use a **solar cell/solar heating panel** to generate electricity. [1 mark]

03.3 You use electricity from the Sun when you need **large/small** amounts of electricity. [1 mark]

03.4 Generating electricity using the Sun **is/is not** reliable, and the devices **are/are not** very expensive to buy. [2 marks]

04 What is the difference between geothermal power and hydroelectric power? Draw lines to link the boxes to make **two** correct sentences. [2 marks]

Hydroelectric power involves pumping water	into the ground where hot rocks turn it to steam	and the steam turns a turbine and generator.

Geothermal power involves pumping water	into a lake, then letting the water fall down	and the water turns a turbine and generator.

05 **Figure 1** is a pie chart that shows the sources we use to generate electricity in the UK.

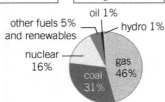

Figure 1

05.1 Calculate the percentage of the UK's electricity that comes from fossil fuels. [2 marks]

_____

_____

HINT Show how you worked out your answer.

05.2 Describe **one** effect that burning fossil fuels has on the environment. [1 mark]

_____

_____

HINT Show how you worked out your answer.

05.3 Name an energy source in **Figure 1** that is in the category 'renewables'. [1 mark]

_____

05.4 Write down **one** advantage and **one** disadvantage of using the energy source named in **05.3**. [2 marks]

_____

_____

06 Dev and Sasha are arguing about which energy resources we should use in the future to generate electricity.
Write down the answer each person would give to the other. Include **two** reasons in each box. [4 marks]

HINT Think about the effect on the environment.

HINT To make two points, use two bullet points.

Dev says: I think we should use nuclear power. It is reliable and doesn't produce greenhouse gases.	**Sasha's reply:**
Sasha says: I think we should use renewables. They are cheaper and better for the environment.	**Dev's reply:**

P3 Checklist

	Student Book	☺	😐	☹
I can describe how most energy demands are met today.	3.1			
I can name the energy resources that are used.	3.1			
I can describe how nuclear fuels are used in power stations.	3.1			
I can name the other fuels that are used to generate electricity.	3.1			
I can describe what a wind turbine is made up of.	3.2			
I can describe how waves can be used to generate electricity.	3.2			
I can name the type of power station that uses water running downhill to generate electricity.	3.2			
I can describe how the tides can be used to generate electricity.	3.2			
I can describe what solar cells are and how they are used.	3.3			
I can describe the difference between a panel of solar cells and a solar heating panel.	3.3			
I can describe what geothermal energy is.	3.3			
I can describe how geothermal energy can be used to generate electricity.	3.3			
I can describe what fossil fuels do to the environment.	3.4			
I can explain why people are concerned about nuclear power.	3.4			
I can describe the advantages and disadvantages of renewable energy resources.	3.4			
I can evaluate the use of different energy resources.	3.4			
I can describe how best to use electricity supplies to meet variations in demand.	3.5			
I can compare the economic costs of different energy resources.	3.5			
I can name energy resources that need to be developed to meet people's energy needs in the future.	3.5			

P4.1 Current and charge

A A circuit diagram shows how the components in a circuit are connected together.

Next to each circuit symbol below, write the name of the circuit component.

Circuit symbol	Component
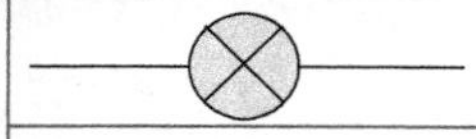 ⊗	
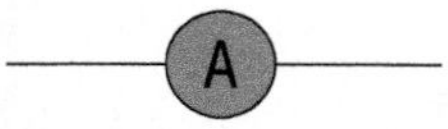 Ⓐ	
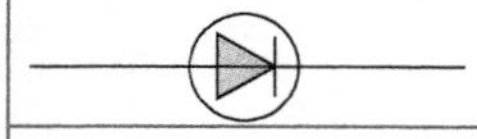 ▷	
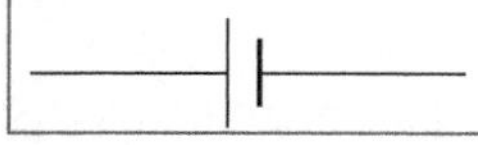 ⊣⊢	

Circuit symbol	Component
 ▭	
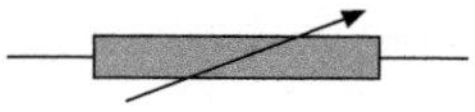 ▱ (arrow)	
 ▭	
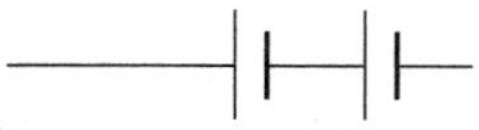 ⊣⊢⊢	

B The following statements are about electric current in circuits.

Tick the boxes to show whether each statement is true or false.

Statement	✓ if true	✓ if false
A current is a flow of **electrons**.		
Charge is measured in amperes.		
Conventional current flows from the negative to the positive terminal of a battery.		
The current before a component is bigger than the current after a component.		
Current is the charge in coulombs flowing per second.		
Current gets smaller further away from the battery.		

C In a torch lamp, a charge of 12 C flows in 2 minutes.

Complete the calculation to find the current:

$$\text{current (A)} = \frac{\text{charge (C)}}{\text{time (s)}}$$

2 min = _____ s

$$\text{current} = \frac{\text{_____} \text{ C}}{\text{_____} \text{ s}}$$

$$= \text{_____ A}$$

What you need to remember

Every circuit component has its own circuit _____, and you use these to draw circuit diagrams.

A battery consists of two or more _____ .

Current is the _____ of flow of charge. You can calculate current using this equation, with units in the brackets:

$$\text{current (\_\_\_)} = \frac{\text{_____ (\_\_\_)}}{\text{_____ (\_\_\_)}}$$

[You need to remember this equation.]

P4.2 Potential difference and resistance

A Which statements about **potential difference** (or **voltage**) are true?

Circle the letters of the true statements.

W Potential difference is the energy transferred to each charge by the battery or cell.

X A bigger potential difference across a bulb means less current flows in the bulb.

Y Potential difference is the energy transferred by each charge to a component.

Z Potential difference is the charge flowing per second.

B These sentences are about Ohm's law and potential difference.

Circle the correct **bold** words and phrases to complete the sentences.

If the current in a component is **directly proportional/inversely proportional** to the potential difference across it, then the component is an ohmic conductor, as long as the **potential difference/temperature** does not change.

If you reverse the potential difference in a circuit, the current **reverses direction/stays the same**.

C A charge of 20 C transfers 240 J of energy as it flows through a resistor.

Complete the calculation to find the potential difference across the resistor.

$$\text{potential difference (V)} = \frac{\text{energy transferred (J)}}{\text{charge (C)}}$$

$$= \frac{\underline{\hspace{2cm}} \text{J}}{\underline{\hspace{2cm}} \text{C}}$$

$$= \underline{\hspace{2cm}} \text{V}$$

D The current through the resistor in activity **C** is 2 A.

Complete the calculation to find the **resistance** of the resistor.

$$\text{resistance } (\Omega) = \frac{\text{potential difference (V)}}{\text{current (A)}}$$

$$= \frac{\underline{\hspace{2cm}} \text{V}}{\underline{\hspace{2cm}} \text{A}}$$

$$= \underline{\hspace{2cm}} \Omega$$

What you need to remember

Potential difference is the _____ transferred to each charge by the battery, or the _____ transferred by each charge to the circuit component. Potential difference is measured in **volts**.

You can calculate potential difference using this equation, with units in the brackets:

$$\text{potential difference (\underline{\hspace{0.5cm}})} = \frac{\underline{\hspace{2cm}} (\underline{\hspace{0.7cm}})}{\underline{\hspace{2cm}} (\underline{\hspace{0.7cm}})}$$

[You need to remember this equation.]

You can calculate resistance (measured in **ohms**) using this equation, with units in the brackets:

$$\text{resistance (\underline{\hspace{0.5cm}})} = \frac{\underline{\hspace{2cm}} (\underline{\hspace{0.7cm}})}{\underline{\hspace{2cm}} (\underline{\hspace{0.7cm}})}$$

[You need to remember this equation.]

Ohm's law says that the current through a resistor is _____ _____ to the potential difference across it. If you reverse the potential difference across a resistor, you _____ the current through it.

P4.3 Component characteristics

A A student wants to take measurements to plot a graph of current against potential difference for a lamp. She has a voltmeter, a bulb, leads, a variable resistor, and a battery.

Write down **one** other component she will need.

_____

B Here are three graphs of current against potential difference. Under each graph, write the name of the component that would produce a graph like this.

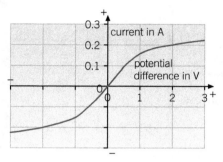 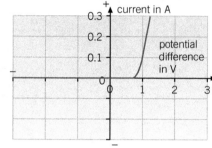 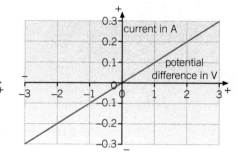

_____   _____   _____

C Complete the table about light-dependent resistors and thermistors by writing one of these words in each box:

hot   **cold**   **light**   **dark**

Device	Has a large resistance when it is ...	Has a small resistance when it is ...
light-dependent resistor		
thermistor		

D You have a circuit with a battery, a bulb, and another circuit component. The bulb is lit. You turn the component around and the bulb goes out.

Complete the sentences.

Name of other component: _____

Why the bulb goes out: _____

_____

_____

What you need to remember

The resistance of a filament bulb _____ if the temperature increases.

For a **diode** the resistance in the forward direction is _____ and the resistance in the reverse direction is _____ . A light-emitting diode (LED) emits light when a current passes through it in the _____ direction.

If the temperature of a thermistor increases, its resistance _____ . If the light intensity on a light-dependent resistor (LDR) increases, its resistance _____ .

P4.4 Series circuits

A Here is a **series** circuit.

a Complete the table about the current in the circuit.

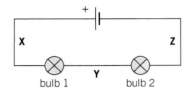

Position	Current in A
X	0.2
Y	
Z	

b Write a sentence to explain how you completed the table.

_____

_____

B In activity **A** the potential difference across bulb 1 is 3 V, and the bulbs are identical.

a Write down the potential difference across bulb 2.

_____

b Write down the potential difference of the cell.

_____

c Write a sentence to explain how you found the answer to part **b**.

_____

_____

C A student makes some changes to the circuit in activity **A**.

Circle the correct **bold** words and phrases below.

If the student adds another bulb to the circuit, the current will be **bigger/smaller/the same**, and the resistance will be **bigger/smaller/the same**.

Two resistors in series have **double/half** the resistance of one resistor.

If the student adds a cell to the battery, the potential difference across the battery will be **double/half**.

What you need to remember

In a series circuit:

- the _____ is the same in each component
- the total _____ _____ is shared between the components
- you find the total resistance by _____ the resistance of all the components.

If you have more than one cell in series, then you _____ all the potential differences to find the total potential difference.

If you add more resistors in series, the total resistance _____. This is because the current through the resistors is _____ but the potential difference across them is the same.

P4.5 Parallel circuits

A Here is a **parallel** circuit.

a Complete the table about the current in the circuit.

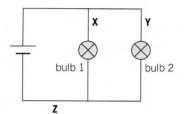

Position	Current in A
X	0.2
Y	
Z	

b Write **two** sentences to explain how you completed the table.

_____

_____

_____

B In activity **A** the potential difference across bulb 1 is 3 V. The bulbs are identical.

a Write down the potential difference across bulb 2. _____

b Write down the potential difference of the cell. _____

C A student makes some changes to the circuit in activity **A**.

Circle the correct **bold** words and phrases below.

If the student adds cell to the battery, the potential difference across the battery will be **double/half**.

If the student adds another bulb to the circuit in parallel, the current at **Z** will be **bigger/smaller/the same**, so the total resistance will be **bigger/smaller/the same**.

Two resistors in parallel would have **double/half** the resistance of one resistor.

What you need to remember

In a parallel circuit:

● the _____ across each component is the same

● you find the total _____ by adding the _____ through each component.

If you use a component that has a bigger resistance, the current through it will be _____ .

You can calculate current using this equation, with units in the brackets:

$$\text{current} \, (\underline{\quad}) = \frac{\underline{\hspace{3cm}} (\underline{\quad})}{\underline{\hspace{2cm}} (\underline{\quad})}$$

[You need to remember this equation.]

If you add more resistors in parallel, the total resistance _____ because the total current _____ but the potential difference is the same.

P4 Practice questions

01 Draw a line to match each quantity to its definition. [2 marks]

potential difference	how easy or hard it is for charge to flow through a component
current	the energy transferred to or by a charge
resistance	the rate of flow of charge

02 Look at the circuit diagram in **Figure 1** and the circuit symbols in **Figure 2**.

Figure 1   **Figure 2**

02.1 Write down the name of component **A**.

_____ [1 mark]

02.2 Write down the name of component **B**.

_____ [1 mark]

02.3 Describe the difference between components **C** and **D**. [1 mark]

_____

_____

02.4 Name a component with a resistance that changes with temperature. [1 mark]

_____

03 A student is looking at two mystery circuits on the bench labelled circuit **A** and circuit **B**.

● Each circuit contains a battery pack, two bulbs, and two switches.

● All of the wires connecting the bulbs to the switches and battery have been covered up by black paper.

● The student knows that each switch is connected next to a bulb.

● All the bulbs are on.

● She knows that one of the circuits is wired in series and the other is wired in parallel.

03.1 Complete the sentences. [2 marks]

The student presses a switch in circuit **A** and only one bulb goes off. This means that circuit **A** is

connected in _____

This happens because _____

_____

_____

03.2 Write down what the student will see if she presses a switch in circuit **B**. [2 marks]

_____

This happens because _____

_____

HINT Think what switches do in series and parallel circuits.

03.3 The resistance of each bulb is 10 Ω. Calculate the resistance of the series circuit. [1 mark]

_____

_____

03.4 Complete the sentences by circling the correct **bold** words and phrases. [3 marks]

In the parallel circuit, the resistance is **bigger/ smaller** than 10 Ω. This is because **less/more** current flows for **a bigger/a smaller/the same** potential difference.

04 There is an electric motor that turns the turntable in a microwave oven.

04.1 A charge of 20 C flows through the motor in 40 seconds. Show that the current is 0.5 A. [2 marks]

_____

_____

HINT Remember, current is charge flowing per second.

04.2 Write down Ohm's law. [2 marks]

_____

_____

04.3 The potential difference across the motor is 12 V. Calculate the resistance. [2 marks]

_____

_____

HINT Think of the models that you have used to help you to remember the equations.

04.4 Write down what would happen to the turntable if the potential difference across the motor was reversed. [1 mark]

_____

P4 Checklist

	Student Book	☺	😐	☹
I can describe how electric circuits are shown as diagrams.	4.1			
I can write down the difference between a battery and a cell.	4.1			
I can describe what determines the size of an electric current.	4.1			
I can calculate the size of an electric current from the charge flow and the time taken.	4.1			
I can write down what is meant by potential difference.	4.2			
I can write down what resistance is and what its unit is.	4.2			
I can write down Ohm's law.	4.2			
I can describe what happens when you reverse the potential difference across a resistor.	4.2			
I can describe what happens to the resistance of a filament lamp as its temperature increases.	4.3			
I can describe how the current through a diode depends on the potential difference across it.	4.3			
I can describe what happens to the resistance of a temperature-dependent resistor as its temperature increases.	4.3			
I can describe what happens to the resistance of a light-dependent resistor as the light level increases.	4.3			
I can describe the current, potential difference, and resistance for each component in a series circuit.	4.4			
I can describe the potential difference of several cells in series.	4.3			
I can calculate the total resistance of two resistors in series.	4.3			
I can explain why adding resistors in series increases the total resistance.	4.3			
I can describe the currents and potential differences for components in a parallel circuit.	4.4			
I can calculate the current through a resistor in a parallel circuit.	4.4			
I can explain why the total resistance of two resistors in parallel is less than the resistance of the smaller individual resistor.	4.4			
I can explain why adding resistors in parallel decreases the total resistance.	4.4			

P5.1 Alternating current

A Draw lines to join the boxes in each column to make **two** correct sentences about current.

| The mains supplies | direct current, | which flows backwards and forwards. |

| A battery supplies | alternating current, | which flows only in one direction. |

B Look at the graph.

Circle the correct **bold** words and phrases to complete the sentences below.

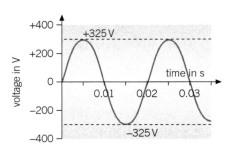

You can work out the peak potential difference (peak p.d.) by finding the **p.d. from zero to the peak/p.d. from the trough to the peak**.

To work out the frequency you first find the time period, which is the **time for half a cycle/time for one cycle**. Then you work out frequency by finding **1 ÷ time period/time period × peak p.d.**

This graph shows the p.d. of the **live/neutral** wire. The p.d. of the **live/neutral** wire is 0 V.

Mains electricity comes to your home through a network of cables and transformers called the National **Grid/Supply**.

C The time period of an alternating supply is 0.2 s.

Complete the calculation to find the frequency of the supply.

$$\text{frequency (Hz)} = \frac{1}{\text{time period (s)}}$$

$$= \frac{1}{\underline{\hspace{2cm}} \text{ s}}$$

$$= \underline{\hspace{2cm}} \text{ Hz}$$

What you need to remember

Direct current (d.c.) flows in _____ direction. Alternating current (a.c.) _____ its direction of flow.

In a mains circuit there is a live wire. Its potential difference alternates between _____ and _____ every cycle. There is also a neutral wire. Its potential difference is _____ volts.

The National Grid is a _____ of cables and transformers that supply electricity to your home.

The peak potential difference of an a.c. supply is the _____ potential difference measured from _____ volts. You can find the frequency of an a.c. supply by measuring the _____ _____, and using the equation:

$$\text{frequency (}\underline{\hspace{1cm}}\text{)} = \frac{1}{\underline{\hspace{2cm}}\ \underline{\hspace{1cm}}\ (\underline{\hspace{1cm}})}$$

P5.2 Cables and plugs

A Colour in or label the diagram of the mains plug to show the colours of the three wires.

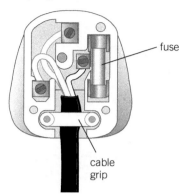

fuse

cable grip

B Draw lines to join the boxes in each column to explain the choice of materials used to make cables and plugs.

The plug casing is made of	soft plastic because	it needs to be an insulator that is flexible.
Each wire is made of	copper because	it needs to be a rigid insulator.
The insulation on the wire is made of	hard plastic because	it needs to conduct electricity.

C Circle the correct **bold** words to complete these sentences about the earth wire.

The earth wire is connected to any **metal/plastic** on the appliance that you can touch. It is also connected to the **longest/shortest** pin of a plug, so that when you plug an appliance in, the case is automatically earthed. If there is a fault and the case is connected to the **live/neutral** wire, the earth wire makes sure you **can/cannot** get a shock if you touch the case.

What you need to remember

Sockets and plugs are made of stiff _____ that encloses electrical connections. This material is used because it is a good _____ .

A mains cable is made up of two or three insulated wires made of _____ surrounded by an outer layer of flexible _____ material.

In a three-pin plug or a three-core cable, the insulation on the live wire is coloured _____ , the neutral wire is coloured _____ , and the earth wire is coloured _____ and _____ .

The earth wire is connected to the _____ pin in a plug. It is used to earth the metal _____ of a mains appliance.

A Draw a box around the correct definition of power.

W Power is the energy transferred per hour.

X Power is the same as energy, but stronger.

Y Power is the energy transferred per second.

Z Power is how efficient a device is.

B An electric car has an electric motor with a power of 15 kW.

Complete the calculation to find the energy transferred during a 1 hour car journey.

energy transferred (J) = power (W) × time (s)

15 kW = _____ W

1 hour = _____ s

energy transferred = _____ W × _____ s

= _____ J

C Complete the calculation to find the electrical power of a mains (230 V) games console. It needs a current of 1.5 A.

power (W) = potential difference (V) × current rating (A)

= _____ V × _____ A

= _____ W

D **a** Complete the calculation to find the current in a mains (230 V) microwave oven that has a power of 1000 W.

$$\text{current (A)} = \frac{\text{power (W)}}{\text{potential difference (V)}}$$

$$\text{current} = \frac{\text{_____ W}}{\text{_____ V}}$$

= _____. A

b The fuses available are 1 A, 3 A, 5 A, and 13 A. Write down the fuse that you need for the microwave oven in part **a**.

_____

What you need to remember

Power is the _____ transferred per second.

You can calculate energy transferred, the power, and the fuse rating using these equations, with units in the brackets:

energy transferred (____) = _____ (____) × _____ (____)

electrical power (____) = _____ _____ (____) × _____ (____)

You can calculate the current, and work out the correct rating for a fuse using this equation, with units in the brackets:

$$\text{fuse rating (\_\_\_\_)} = \frac{\text{_____ (\_\_\_\_)}}{\text{_____ _____ (\_\_\_\_)}}$$

[You need to remember these equations.]

P5.4 Electrical currents and energy transfer

A Tick the statement that correctly explains why a resistor in a circuit gets hot.

Statement	✓ if correct explanation
The potential difference flowing through the resistor heats it up.	
The electrons that make up the current heat up.	
The electrons transfer energy to the resistor and heat it up.	

B You might sometimes have felt a small shock from a car door handle. When this happens a current of about 4 mA flows for about 0.1 s.

Complete the calculation to find the charge that flows.

charge (C) = current (A) × time (s)

4 mA = _____ A

charge = _____ A × _____ s

= _____ C

C Complete these sentences by circling the correct **bold** words and phrases.

The potential difference (p.d.) tells you the **energy/power** transferred to or by each charge.

A bigger p.d. means each charge transfers **less/more** energy in the electrical component or device.

In an electric circuit with a battery supplying 6 J of energy per charge, the energy supplied to the components in the circuit will be **less than 6 J/more than 6 J/6 J** for each charge that flows.

D When you use a toaster the wire inside the toaster heats up. The toaster is connected to the mains at 230 V, and a charge of 300 000 C flows.

Complete the calculation to find the energy transferred.

energy transferred (J) = charge (C) × potential difference (V)

energy transferred = _____ C × _____ V

= _____ J

What you need to remember

You can calculate charge flow and the energy transferred using these equations, with units in the brackets:

charge (____) = _____ (____) × _____ (____)

energy (____) = _____ _____ (____) × _____ (____)

[You need to remember these equations.]

When charge flows through a resistor, the energy transferred makes the resistor _____ .

When charge flows around a circuit, the _____ supplied by the battery is equal to the _____ transferred to all the components in the circuit.

P5.5 Appliances and efficiency

A a Circle the **two** quantities below that you need to know to calculate the power of an electrical appliance.

   potential difference   **type of appliance**   **current**   **cost**

b Write down the other quantity that you need to know to calculate the energy transferred to the appliance.

   _____

B Jules uses an electric oven to cook a chicken. The oven needs a potential difference of 230 V and has a current flowing through it of 15 A.

Complete the calculation to find the power of the oven. Write your answer to 2 significant figures.

power (W) = potential difference (V) × current (A)

   power = _____ V × _____ A

   = _____ W = _____ W to 2 significant figures

C It takes 30 minutes to cook a pizza in an oven with a power of 2000 W.

Complete the calculation to find the energy transferred.

energy transferred (J) = power (W) × time (s)

   30 minutes = _____ s

   energy transferred = _____ W × _____ s

   = _____ J

D Another oven is 70% efficient. It supplies 4000 kJ.

Complete the calculation to find the useful energy.

useful energy (J) = efficiency × energy supplied (J)

   70% efficient = _____ as a decimal fraction

   4000 kJ = _____ J

   useful energy = _____ × _____ J

   = _____ J

What you need to remember

A domestic meter measures how much _____ is transferred to appliances in your home.

You can calculate the energy supplied to an appliance using this equation, with units in the brackets:

energy supplied (____) = _____ (____) × _____ (____)

useful energy (____) = _____ × _____ (____)

[You need to remember these equations.]

P5 Practice questions

01 Label the diagram of the plug (**Figure 1**) with the colours of the wires. [3 marks]

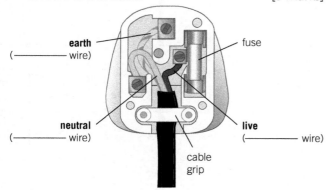

Figure 1

02 **Table 1** shows some information about three wires in a plug.

Table 1

Wire	Statement
A	connected to the metal casing of an appliance
B	at 230 V
C	at 0 V

02.1 Write down the letter of the earth wire.

_____ [1 mark]

02.2 Write down the letter of the neutral wire.

_____ [1 mark]

02.3 Write down the letter of the live wire. _____
[1 mark]

02.4 Write down the letters of the **two** wires that make a complete circuit with an appliance.

_____ [1 mark]

02.5 Write down the name of the network of wires and transformers to which the plug is connected.

_____ [1 mark]

03.1 Choose the most appropriate material for the outside of the plug by circling **one** of the materials below. [1 mark]

copper   hard plastic   aluminium   soft plastic

03.2 Write down **one** reason for your choice in **03.1**.
[1 mark]

_____

03.3 Choose the most appropriate material for the outside of wires in a plug by circling **one** of the materials below. [1 mark]

copper   hard plastic   aluminium   soft plastic

03.4 Write down **one** reason for your choice in **03.3**.
[1 mark]

_____

04 A student has some hair straighteners. The label says: 1100 W, 230 V. Calculate the fuse that she needs to use in the plug. The fuses available are 3 A, 5 A, and 13 A. [4 marks]

_____

_____

_____

_____

HINT You need to use a fuse rated as close to the current as possible, but bigger.

05 A student does a survey of the appliances in her kitchen. **Table 2** shows the results. All the appliances work on a potential difference of 230 V (the mains).

Table 2

Appliance	Power rating in W	Current in A
kettle	1200	5.2
microwave	800	3.5
refrigerator	420	1.8
toaster	1000	4.4

05.1 Calculate the energy transferred when you microwave popcorn for 2 minutes. [3 marks]

_____

_____

05.2 Write a sentence to explain why the wires inside the toaster get hot. [2 marks]

_____

_____

05.3 Calculate the charge that flows through a kettle during the 6 minutes that it takes to boil. Give your answer to 2 significant figures. [3 marks]

_____

_____

HINT Remember that significant figures are not the same as decimal places.

05.4 The refrigerator is on all day and all night. Calculate the energy transferred in one day. Give your answer to 2 significant figures. [3 marks]

_____

_____

HINT You need to convert 24 hours into seconds.

P5 Checklist

	Student Book	☺	☺	☹
I can write down what direct current is and what alternating current is.	5.1			
I can describe what is meant by the live wire and the neutral wire of a mains circuit.	5.1			
I can describe the National Grid.	5.1			
I can describe how to use an oscilloscope to measure the frequency and peak potential difference of an alternating current.	5.1			
I can describe what the casing of a mains plug or socket is made of and explain why.	5.2			
I can write down what is in a mains cable.	5.2			
I can write down the colours of the live, neutral, and earth wires.	5.2			
I can explain why a three-pin plug includes an earth pin.	5.2			
I can describe how power and energy are related	5.3			
I can use the power rating of an appliance to calculate the energy transferred in a given time.	5.3			
I can calculate the electrical power supplied to a device from its current and potential difference.	5.3			
I can work out the correct fuse to use in an appliance.	5.3			
I can calculate the flow of electric charge given the current and time.	5.4			
I can write down the energy transfers when electric charge flows through a resistor.	5.4			
I can describe how the energy transferred by a flow of electric charge is related to potential difference.	5.4			
I can link the electrical energy supplied by the battery in a circuit to the energy transferred to the electrical components.	5.4			
I can calculate the energy supplied to an electrical appliance from its current, its potential difference, and how long it is used for.	5.5			
I can work out the useful energy output of an electrical appliance.	5.5			
I can work out the output power of an electrical appliance.	5.5			
I can compare different appliances that do the same job.	5.5			

P6.1 Density

A Complete the calculation to find the **density** of a person with a mass of 70 kg and a volume of 0.07 m³.

$$\text{density (kg/m}^3) = \frac{\text{mass (kg)}}{\text{volume (m}^3)}$$

$$= \frac{\underline{\hspace{2cm}} \text{ kg}}{\underline{\hspace{2cm}} \text{ m}^3}$$

$$= \underline{\hspace{2cm}} \text{ kg/m}^3$$

B These phrases describe some objects and some measurements taken to find their density.

Draw lines to make a correct sentence for each object.

To find the density of a regular solid, such as a brick,	you measure the mass of an empty and full measuring cylinder	and measure the volume of water it displaces.
To find the density of a liquid, such as water,	you use a digital balance to find the mass	and measure the volume with a measuring cylinder.
To find the density of an irregular solid, such as a stone,	you use a digital balance to find the mass	and measure the volume with a ruler.

C Tick the correct statement about objects floating in water.

Statement	✓ if correct
Only light objects such as a plastic ball float on water.	
An object floats if its density is less than that of water.	
An object floats if its density is more than that of water.	

What you need to remember

Density depends on _____ and _____, and is measured in _____ .

You can calculate density using this equation, with units in the brackets:

$$\text{density (kg/m}^3) = \frac{\underline{\hspace{2cm}} (\underline{\hspace{1cm}})}{\underline{\hspace{2cm}} (\underline{\hspace{1cm}})}$$

[You need to remember this equation.]

From this you can work out that mass = _____ × _____ , and volume = _____

You use a digital balance to measure _____ , and a ruler or measuring cylinder to measure _____ .

An object will float on water if its density is _____ _____ that of water.

P6.2 States of matter

A Draw a line to match each state to its correct description.

State

| solid |
| liquid |
| gas |

Description

| Particles move about randomly and are far apart. |
| Particles are held next to each other in fixed positions. |
| Particles move at random and are in contact with each other. |

B Draw lines to make **six** correct sentences about changes of state. You will need to use some of the phrases more than once.

| condenses to form |

| A solid |
| A liquid |
| A gas |

| vaporises or boils to form |
| melts to form |
| solidifies or freezes to form |
| sublimates to form |

| a gas. |
| a liquid. |
| a solid. |

C Circle the correct **bold** words and phrases in the sentences below.

A substance in a gas state is the **least/most** energetic, and a substance in a solid state is the **least/most** energetic.

When a substance changes from one state to another its mass **does/does not** change, because the number of particles **does/does not** change.

A change of state is a physical change because new substances **are/are not** formed.

What you need to remember

In a _____ the particles move about randomly and are far apart. In a _____ the particles move at random and are in contact with each other. In a _____ the particles are held next to each other in fixed positions.

A _____ is the least energetic state of matter, and a _____ is the most energetic state of matter.

When a substance changes state, the _____ stays the same because the number of particles stays the same.

P6.3 Changes of state

A Jo took some ice out of the freezer and put it on a plate in a warm room.
This graph shows what happened to the temperature of the ice over time.

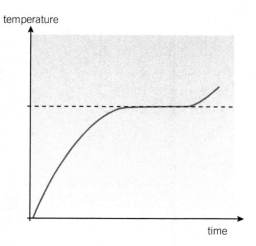

Label the diagram using the words below.

melting point   **liquid**   **solid + liquid**   **solid**

B Jo then reversed the process by putting the melted ice back in the freezer.

Complete the sentences below using the following words and phrases.

freezing point   **horizontal**   **latent heat**

The temperature–time graph would be _____ during the time that the water is changing to ice. This

temperature is the _____ _____ of water. The energy transferred to the surroundings of the

freezer when this happens is called the _____ _____.

C Tick the boxes to show whether each statement is true for boiling or evaporation.
You may need to tick **both** boxes for some statements.

Statement	✓ if true for boiling	✓ if true for evaporation
This process happens at the **boiling point** of the liquid.		
The mass does not change.		
The particles escape only from the surface of the liquid.		
This process happens at or below the boiling point of the liquid.		

What you need to remember

The melting point of a pure substance is the temperature at which it _____ or _____ , and the

boiling point is the temperature at which it _____ or _____ .

You can find the melting point or boiling point from the _____ section of a temperature–time graph.

_____ occurs throughout a liquid at its boiling point, but _____ occurs from the surface of a liquid

at a temperature below its boiling point.

P6.4 Internal energy

A Tick **all** the descriptions of energy that apply to the **internal energy** of a substance in different states.

Energy	✓ if included in internal energy
the kinetic energy of the particles in a gas	
the energy of vibration of the particles in a solid	
the gravitational potential energy of the particles in a liquid	
the kinetic energy of a whole solid	

B Draw a line to match each sentence start with an ending to make **three** correct sentences.

If you heat a substance	the potential energy of the particles increases.
If you heat a substance and its temperature changes	its internal energy increases.
If you heat a substance and its temperature does not change	the kinetic energy of the particles increases.

C Circle the correct **bold** words in the sentences below.

To melt 1 kg of a solid substance, you need to transfer **less/more** energy to it than you would need to boil 1 kg of this substance in the liquid state. This is because the forces of attraction between the particles in the solid state are **stronger/weaker** than the forces of attraction between the particles in the liquid state. It takes **less/more** energy to break the bonds between the particles in the solid state than it does to break the bonds in the liquid state.

D Write a sentence to explain why a gas exerts a pressure on the surfaces that enclose it.

_____

_____

What you need to remember

If the temperature of a substance increases, its internal energy _____ .

The strength of the forces of _____ between the particles explains why a substance is a solid, liquid, or gas.

If you heat a substance and its temperature rises, the _____ energy of its particles increases. If you heat a substance and its temperature *does not* rise, the _____ energy of its particles increases.

The pressure of a gas on a surface is caused by the particles of the gas repeatedly _____ with the surface.

P6.5 Specific latent heat

A Tick the boxes to show whether each description is true for latent heat and for specific latent heat.

Description	✓ if true for latent heat	✓ if true for specific latent heat
measured in joules		
energy to change the state of 1 kg of a substance		
measured in J/kg		
energy to change the state of a substance		

B Sort these sentences into the correct order to describe how to measure the **specific latent heat of vaporisation** of water.

Write the letters in order below.

P Look at the joulemeter to record the energy transferred by the heater during the 10 minutes.

Q Turn the heater on for 10 minutes and measure the mass again.

R Put water in a beaker with a heater, put the beaker on a digital balance, and measure the mass.

S Find the difference in the two masses of water, and use the equation specific latent heat = energy/mass to find the specific latent heat.

Correct order: _____

C A student wanted to measure the thermal energy needed to melt ice. He measured the mass of some ice. He melted the ice and measured the mass of the water. The **specific latent heat of fusion** of ice is 334 kJ/kg, and the mass of water melted was 0.03 kg. Give your answer to three significant figures.

Complete the calculation to find the thermal energy for this change of state.

thermal energy for melting ice (J) = specific latent heat of fusion (J/kg) × mass (kg)

$$334 \text{ kJ/kg} = \text{_____} \text{ J/kg}$$

thermal energy for melting ice = _____ J/kg × _____ kg

$$= \text{_____} \text{ J}$$

What you need to remember

Latent heat is the _____ you need to transfer to a substance to change its state without changing its

_____ .

Specific latent heat of fusion or vaporisation is the energy you need to transfer to a substance to melt or boil a

mass of _____ of the substance without changing its _____ .

You can calculate the energy transferred using this equation, with units in the brackets:

thermal energy for a change of state (_____) = _____ (_____) × _____ _____ _____ (_____)

You can measure the specific latent heat of ice or water using a low-voltage heater to _____ the ice, or to _____ the water.

P6.6 Gas pressure and temperature

A Tick the boxes to show whether each statement about gas molecules and temperature is true or false.

When you heat a gas...	✓ if true	✓ if false
... the average speed of the gas molecules increases.		
... the molecules get hotter.		
... the molecules get bigger.		
... the molecules collide more often with the surface that encloses the gas.		

B Molly carried out an investigation into the relationship between temperature and pressure. Here is the graph that she plotted from her results.

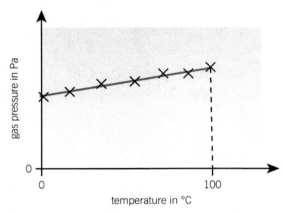

Circle the correct **bold** words in the sentences below.

As the temperature increases the pressure of the gas **decreases/increases** because:

● the molecules collide **less/more** often with the surface of the container that encloses it
● when the molecules do collide with the container they exert **less/more** force.

C Write a sentence to describe a piece of evidence for the motion of gas molecules.

_____

_____

_____

_____

What you need to remember

Gas molecules colliding with the surfaces in contact with the gas cause gas _____ .

If the temperature of a gas in a sealed container increases, the pressure _____ because:

● there are _____ impacts per second
● the force of the impacts _____ .

You can see evidence for the _____ motion of gas molecules by observing smoke particles.

01 Circle the correct unit of density. [1 mark]

N **m³** **N/m²** **kg/m³** **kg/m²**

02 Write down the name of the change of state in the following situations. [3 marks]

02.1 a solid changing to a liquid _____

02.2 a gas changing to a liquid _____

02.3 a solid changing to a gas _____

03 You have a sealed flask full of air connected to a pressure gauge. Complete the sentences below, choosing from the following words. You do not need to use all the words.

pressure   **collide**   **faster**   **slower**

less   **more**   **increase**   **decrease**

03.1 The air molecules inside the flask _____ with the inside surfaces, and exert a _____ on them. [2 marks]

03.2 If you put the flask in hot water the pressure will _____ . This is because the gas molecules will move _____ and collide _____ often with the surfaces. [3 marks]

04 **Figure 1** shows a graph of the temperature of a liquid as it is heated.

Figure 1

04.1 Write down the boiling point of the liquid.

_____ [1 mark]

04.2 Describe what happens to the molecules in the first 5 minutes of heating.

_____

_____

_____

[3 marks]

HINT Remember that a horizontal section of the graph means that the temperature is not changing.

05 You have 0.5 m³ cubes of three types of solid material: **A**, **B**, and **C**. **Table 1** shows the masses of the cubes.

Table 1

Material	Mass in kg
A	2000
B	3700
C	3000

05.1 Write down the letter of the material that has the highest density. _____ [1 mark]

HINT Think about the definition of density.

05.2 Calculate the density of the material with the lowest density. [3 marks]

_____

_____

06 Sort these steps into the correct order to describe how to measure the specific latent heat of fusion of ice. Write the letters in order below. [4 marks]

A Look at the joulemeter to record the energy transferred by the heater during the 10 minutes.

B Turn the heater on.

C Allow the ice to melt for 10 minutes and measure the mass of water collected.

D Put ice in a funnel, put the funnel in a beaker on a digital balance, and put a heater into the ice, but do not turn it on.

E Use the equation specific latent heat = energy/mass of water collected, to find the specific latent heat.

Correct order: _____

07 An ice cube of mass 2 g melts, and the water heats up to room temperature, which is 20 °C.

The specific latent heat of melting of ice is 334 000 J/kg, and the specific heat capacity of water is 4200 J/kg °C.

Calculate the total energy supplied to the ice cube. Use these equations:

thermal energy for a change of state = mass × specific latent heat

change in thermal energy = mass × specific heat capacity × temperature change [4 marks]

_____

_____

_____

_____

_____

HINT Work out the energy supplied to melt the ice cube, then the energy supplied to raise the temperature of that mass of water from 0 °C to 20 °C.

P6 Checklist

	Student Book	☺	😐	☹
I can define density and write down its unit.	6.1			
I can describe how to measure the density of a solid object or a liquid.	6.1			
I can use the density equation to calculate the mass or the volume of an object or a sample.	6.1			
I can describe how to tell from its density if an object will float in water.	6.1			
I can describe the different properties of solids, liquids, and gases.	6.2			
I can describe the arrangement of particles in a solid, a liquid, and a gas.	6.2			
I can explain why gases are less dense than solids and liquids.	6.2			
I can explain why the mass of a substance that changes state stays the same.	6.2			
I can write down what the melting point and the boiling point of a substance mean.	6.3			
I can describe what you need to do to melt a solid or to boil a liquid.	6.3			
I can explain the difference between boiling and evaporation.	6.3			
I can use a temperature–time graph to find the melting point or the boiling point of a substance.	6.3			
I can describe how increasing the temperature of a substance affects its internal energy.	6.4			
I can explain the different properties of a solid, a liquid, and a gas.	6.4			
I can describe how the energy of the particles of a substance changes when it is heated.	6.4			
I can explain in terms of particles why a gas exerts pressure.	6.4			
I can write down what latent heat means as a substance changes its state.	6.5			
I can write down what specific latent heat of fusion and of vaporisation mean.	6.5			
I can use specific latent heat in calculations.	6.5			
I can describe how to measure the specific latent heat of ice and of water.	6.5			
I can describe how a gas exerts pressure on a surface.	6.6			
I can describe how changing the temperature of a gas in a sealed container affects the pressure of the gas.	6.6			
I can explain why raising the temperature of a gas in a sealed container increases the pressure of the gas.	6.6			
I can describe how to see evidence of gas molecules moving around at random.	6.6			

P7.1 Atoms and radiation

A Circle the **three** main types of radiation emitted by an unstable nucleus.

beta   radio   gamma   infrared   alpha

B Tick the **three** statements about radioactivity that are correct.

	Statement	✓ if correct
P	Radioactivity is the name of the property of materials that emit radiation.	
Q	The particles or waves that stable nuclei emit are called radiation.	
R	If something is random, you can predict when it will happen.	
S	A nucleus that emits radiation is unstable.	
T	A nucleus that does not emit radiation is random.	

Write corrected versions of the two statements that are incorrect.

_____

_____

_____

_____

C Draw a line to match each radiation to the material that stops it and to its symbol.

Radiation	Stopped by	Symbol
alpha radiation	lead	α
beta radiation	paper	β
gamma radiation	aluminium	γ

What you need to remember

A radioactive substance contains _____ nuclei that usually become

_____ after emitting radiation.

Radioactive sources emit three main types of radiation: _____, _____, and

_____ .

You cannot predict when a nucleus will emit radiation, so we say radioactive decay is _____ .

P7.2 The discovery of the nucleus

A Look at the diagram of Rutherford's experiment with alpha particles.

Circle the correct **bold** words in the sentences below.

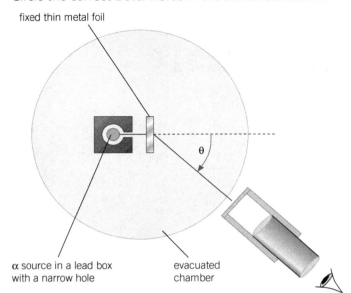

fixed thin metal foil

θ

α source in a lead box
with a narrow hole

evacuated
chamber

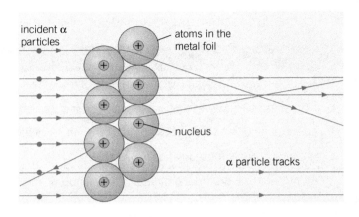

incident α
particles

atoms in the
metal foil

nucleus

α particle tracks

Rutherford used **alpha/beta** particles to probe atoms. He put a thin **metal/plastic** foil in a chamber with no air
and fired the particles at the foil. Most of the particles **came back/went through** but some **came back/went
through**. He said that most of the mass was concentrated **in the middle/on the outside** of the atom in a very small
negatively/positively charged nucleus.

B The other model of the atom at the time was the 'plum pudding' model.

Draw lines to match the sentence starts and endings below to explain why the model of the atom changed.

If the 'plum pudding' model were correct	they do not explain experimental observations.
Models are rejected if	either all the particles would go through, or all of them would come back.
The 'plum pudding' model could not explain why	some particles were scattered through large angles.

What you need to remember

Rutherford used _____ particles to probe atoms. He fired them at a thin metal foil and
discovered that most of them went through, but some were scattered by _____ angles.
He could not explain this scattering using the _____ _____ model.
Rutherford's model said that most of the mass of the atom is in a _____ ,
_____ charged nucleus in the centre of an atom.

P7.3 Changes in the nucleus

A a Here are some symbols for atoms.

Circle the **two** isotopes of the same element.

$^{14}_{6}C$　　$^{14}_{7}N$　　$^{12}_{6}C$　　$^{16}_{8}C$

b Complete the sentence below:

Isotopes of an element are made up of atoms that have _____

_____

_____

B Tick the statements about alpha and beta decay that are correct.

Statement	✓ if correct
In alpha decay a nucleus loses two protons and two neutrons.	
In beta decay a nucleus loses two protons and two neutrons.	
In alpha decay a nucleus gains two protons and two neutrons.	
In beta decay a neutron changes into a proton and an electron.	

C Here are some sentences about what happens when an unstable nucleus decays.

W Neither the **atomic mass** nor the **atomic number** changes.

X The atomic number goes up by 1 and the atomic mass does not change.

Y The atomic number goes down by 2 and the atomic mass goes down by 4.

Z The atomic number does not change and the atomic mass goes down by 1.

a Write down the letter that describes what happens in alpha decay.

_____

b Write down the letter that describes what happens in beta decay.

_____

What you need to remember

Isotopes of an element are atoms with the _____ number of protons but a _____ number of neutrons. They have the _____ atomic number but _____ mass numbers.

When a nucleus emits an alpha particle it loses _____ protons and _____ neutrons. The mass number goes down by _____, and the atomic number goes down by _____ .

When a nucleus emits a beta particle a _____ changes to a _____ and emits an _____ . The mass number _____ _____, and the atomic number goes up by _____ .

P7.4 More about alpha, beta, and gamma radiation

A Unstable atoms may emit alpha, beta, or gamma radiation.

Label the diagram by writing a type of radiation in each space.

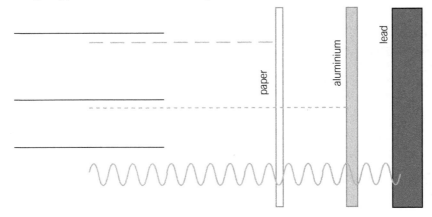

B Colour the boxes to link the parts and make **three** correct sentences about the radiation emitted from unstable atoms. You should use one colour for each sentence.

Alpha radiation	has an infinite range in air,	consists of a fast-moving electron,	and is the most ionising.
Beta radiation	has a range of about 1 m in air,	consists of two protons and two neutrons,	and is moderately ionising.
Gamma radiation	has a range of a few cm in air,	consists of electromagnetic radiation,	and is the least ionising.

C Write **two** sentences to describe what happens when ionising radiation passes through the human body.

_____

_____

_____

What you need to remember

Alpha radiation is stopped by _____ , beta radiation is stopped by _____ , and gamma radiation is stopped by _____ .

In air alpha radiation has a range of _____ , beta radiation has a range of _____ , and gamma radiation has an _____ range.

An alpha particle consists of _____ protons and _____ neutrons, a beta particle is a _____-moving _____ , and gamma radiation is _____ radiation.

Alpha radiation is the _____ ionising, and gamma radiation is the _____ ionising.

All three types of radiation _____ substances as they pass through them, which can _____ or kill living cells.

P7.5 Activity and half-life

A Draw a line to match each term to its definition.

count rate	the number of decays per second
activity	the number of counts per second on a Geiger counter
becquerel	the unit of activity

B Tick **all** of the correct definitions of **half-life**.

Definition	✓ if correct
Half-life is the time for the number of alpha particles to halve.	
Half-life is the time for the number of unstable nuclei to halve.	
Half-life is the time for the activity to halve.	
Half-life is the time for the amount of radiation to halve.	

C Look at the graph.

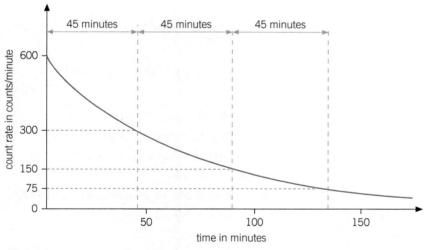

Circle the correct **bold** word and phrases in these sentences.

The half-life of the isotope is **45/90/135** minutes. A graph of the number of unstable nuclei against time would have **a different/the same** shape as this graph. A count rate of 1 count per minute is **bigger than/equal to/ smaller than** one becquerel.

What you need to remember

The half-life of a radioactive isotope is the average time it takes for the number of nuclei of the isotope to

_____ .

The count rate of a Geiger counter decreases as the activity of a radioactive source _____ .

In one half-life, the activity and the number of atoms of a radioactive isotope will _____ .

P7 Practice questions

01 There are three types of radiation that can be emitted by an unstable nucleus.

Tick the boxes in **Table 1** to show whether each property is true for each type of radiation.   [6 marks]

Table 1

Property	✓ if true for alpha	✓ if true for beta	✓ if true for gamma
is stopped by paper			
has the symbol β			
travels only a few centimetres in air			
is stopped only by lead and concrete			
has the symbol γ			
travels only about 1 m in air			

02 Here are some statements about what happens to the atomic mass and atomic number of a nucleus that decays. Write a possible type of decay for each statement.

02.1 The mass number goes down by four:

_____

02.2 The mass number does not change:

_____

02.3 The atomic number goes up by one:

_____   [3 marks]

03 Ideas about the atom have changed over time.

Here are three descriptions of models of atoms.

A   a positively charged sphere with negatively charged electrons embedded in it

B   a positively charged nucleus with electrons in specific energy levels around it

C   a positively charged nucleus with electrons in orbit around it

Write down the letter that matches each model: [3 marks]

03.1 the model that we use now _____

03.2 the model that scientists thought was accurate before Rutherford's scattering experiment

_____

03.3 the model that scientists thought was accurate after Rutherford's scattering experiment. _____ .

04 Write down the **observation** from Rutherford's scattering experiment that led to the change in the model.   [2 marks]

_____

_____

05 **Figure 1** shows a graph of the activity of a radioactive sample against time.

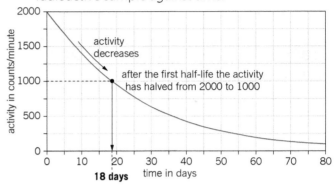

Figure 1

Decide whether each statement below is correct based on the information in the graph.

Write the letters of the correct statements.

[2 marks]

A   After 36 days the activity will be zero.

B   The graph shows that the activity of the sample is decreasing, which means that the number of unstable nuclei is increasing.

C   The number of unstable nuclei halves in 18 days.

D   The half-life of this sample is 18 days.

Letters of correct statements:

_____

HINT   The half-life is the time for the activity to halve.

06 A radiographer in a hospital is preparing a sample of technetium-99. She shields herself from the radiation that the technetium emits.

06.1 Explain why radiation is hazardous to the human body.   [1 mark]

_____

_____

06.2 Complete the nuclear equation for the beta decay of technetium-101.   [2 marks]

$$^{101}_{43}\text{Tc} \rightarrow \boxed{}_{\boxed{}}\text{Ru} + \,^{0}_{-1}\beta$$

HINT   Remember that the top number is the mass number, and the bottom number is the atomic number.

P7 Checklist

	Student Book	☺	☺	☹
I can write down what a radioactive substance is.	7.1			
I can write down the types of radiation given out from a radioactive substance.	7.1			
I can write down what happens when a radioactive source emits radiation (radioactive decay).	7.1			
I can write down the different types of radiation emitted by radioactive sources.	7.1			
I can describe how the nuclear model of the atom was established.	7.2			
I can explain why the 'plum pudding' model of the atom was rejected.	7.2			
I can describe what conclusions were made about the atom from experimental evidence.	7.2			
I can explain why the nuclear model was accepted.	7.2			
I can write down what an isotope is.	7.3			
I can describe how the nucleus of an atom changes when it emits an alpha particle or a beta particle.	7.3			
I can represent the emission of an alpha particle from a nucleus.	7.3			
I can represent the emission of a beta particle from a nucleus.	7.3			
I can write down how far each type of radiation can travel in air.	7.4			
I can describe how different materials absorb alpha, beta, and gamma radiation.	7.4			
I can describe the ionising power of alpha, beta, and gamma radiation.	7.4			
I can explain why alpha, beta, and gamma radiation are dangerous.	7.4			
I can write down what the half-life of a radioactive source means.	7.5			
I can describe what happens to the count rate from a radioactive isotope as it decays.	7.5			

P8.1 Vectors and scalars

A Physical quantities are scalars or vectors.

Tick the boxes to show whether each description applies to a scalar quantity or a vector quantity, or tick **both** boxes if it applies to both.

Description	✓ if it applies to a scalar quantity	✓ if it applies to a vector quantity
has **magnitude**		
has direction		
can be represented by an arrow		

B Circle the vectors in the list below.

distance   force   time   velocity   acceleration   speed

C Choose the best definition of **displacement** below.

Circle the letter of your chosen definition.

W the distance from home

X the distance travelled

Y the distance travelled in a certain direction

Z speed × time

D Draw an arrow on the diagram to represent the force of the hammer on the nail.

What you need to remember

Displacement is the _____ in a given direction.

A vector quantity is a physical quantity that has _____ and _____ . A scalar quantity is a physical quantity that has _____ only.

You can represent a vector quantity with an arrow. The direction of the arrow tells you the _____ of the vector, and the length of the arrow tells you the _____ of the vector.

P8.2 Forces between objects

A A force is a push or a pull.

Draw a line to match each sentence start to the correct ending to make **three** correct sentences about forces.

A force can change the shape of an object, for example,		a tennis ball hitting the ground.

A force can change the motion of an object, for example,		a rocket taking off.

A force can start an object moving that was at rest, for example,		accelerating on a bicycle.

B Tick the boxes to show whether each **force** is a contact force or a non-contact force.

Force	✓ if it is a contact force	✓ if it is a non-contact force
friction		
electrostatic		
gravity		
air resistance		
tension		
magnetic		

C Complete the sentences by circling the correct **bold** words and phrases below.

Newton's third law says that two objects that interact exert **different/equal** and opposite forces, measured in newtons, on each other. This means that the Earth is pulling you with a **frictional/gravitational** force, and you are pulling the Earth with a force that is **bigger/smaller/the same size**.

The driving force that an engine produces is due to **friction/gravity**. One of the forces that opposes the motion of a moving car is **friction/gravity**.

What you need to remember

Forces can change the _____ of an object, change the _____ of an object, or start a _____ object moving. Forces are measured in _____ .

A _____ force is a force that acts on objects only when they touch each other.

When two objects interact they always exert _____ and _____ forces on each other.

P8.3 Resultant forces

A Several forces may act on an object.

Write down what **resultant force** means.

_____

_____

_____

B Tick the boxes to show whether each statement about resultant forces is true or false.

Statement	✓ if true	✓ if false
If there is no resultant force on a stationary object it will not move.		
If there is a resultant force on an object that is moving with a steady speed it will always speed up.		
If there is a resultant force on an object that is not moving, then it will move with a steady speed.		
If there is no resultant force on an object that is moving with a steady speed, then it will slow down.		
If there is a resultant force on an object that is moving with a steady speed, then it may change direction.		

C The table shows some pairs of forces that act along the same line.

Complete the table by finding the resultant force of each pair of forces.

Write the magnitude and the direction (left or right).

Force to the left in N	Force to the right in N	Resultant force magnitude in N	Resultant force direction (left or right?)
7	3		
10	20		
80	150		

> ### What you need to remember
>
> The resultant force is a single force that has the _____ effect as all the forces acting on an object.
>
> An object stays at rest or moves with a steady speed when the resultant force on it is _____ .
>
> The speed or direction of an object changes when the resultant force on it is _____ than
>
> _____ .
>
> If there are two forces acting on an object along the same line you _____ them if they act in the same direction, and find the _____ if they act in opposite directions.

P8.4 Centre of mass

A Car designers keep the centre of mass of a car near to the ground.

Choose the correct definition for the centre of mass.

W The centre of mass is a point that is always at the bottom of the object.

X The centre of mass is a point that is always in the middle of the object.

Y The centre of mass is the point where you can imagine all the mass is concentrated.

Z The centre of mass is the point where all the forces on the object would be zero.

B Put a dot in each object below where you expect its centre of mass to be.

C The diagram shows an experiment to find the centre of mass of an object.

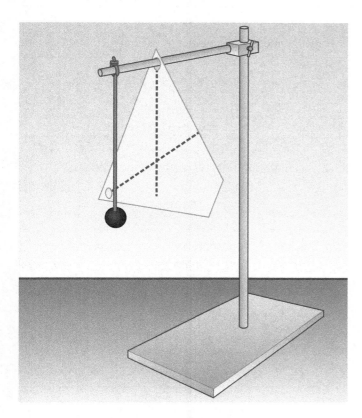

Circle the correct **bold** words below.

If you suspend an object, you know that the centre of mass lies on a line **above/below** the point of suspension.

If you draw a line from two suspension points, the centre of mass is where the lines **cross/separate**.

What you need to remember

The centre of mass of an object is the _____ where all the mass is concentrated.

For a uniform object such as a sphere or a cube, the centre of mass is in the _____ of the object.

A suspended object will stop swinging when the centre of mass is _____ the point of suspension.

The centre of mass of a symmetrical object is along its _____ of symmetry.

P8 Practice questions

01 **Table 1** gives some descriptions of position and motion. Tick to show which of them describe vector quantities. [2 marks]

Table 1

Position or motion	✓ if vector
4 m	
30 m north	
2 m/s south	
5 m/s	

02 Circle the contact forces in the list below. [2 marks]

gravity   **friction**   **tension**

magnetic attraction   **air resistance**

03 A resultant force can change the direction of motion of an object.

03.1 Write down **one** other thing that a resultant force can do. [1 mark]

_____

_____

03.2 **Figure 1** shows some forces acting on a box. Draw an arrow (where appropriate) above each box to show the resultant force acting on the box. Label the arrow with the magnitude of the force. [3 marks]

Figure 1

04 Max is sitting on a chair. He gets up and stands on the floor.

Complete the sentences by circling the correct **bold** words and phrases.

04.1 When Max is sitting on the chair, the downwards force is the force of the **chair/Earth** on him, and the upwards force is the force of the **chair/Earth/upthrust** on him. [2 marks]

04.2 When Max is standing, the force of the Earth on him is **bigger than/smaller than/the same as** it was in part **04.1**. [1 mark]

04.3 According to Newton's third law, in the interaction between Max and the Earth, Max pulls on the Earth with a force that is **much smaller than/the same size as** the force of the Earth pulling on him.

[1 mark]

05 A resultant force can change the motion of an object. **Table 2** describes objects and the forces acting on them. In the final column, write down what the object will start to do. [4 marks]

Table 2

What the object is doing	Resultant force	What the object will start to do
not moving	2 N to the right	
moving at 3 m/s to the left	none	
moving at 3 m/s to the left	2 N to the right	
not moving	none	

06 A girl pushes a toy car on a grid. She moves it the following distances: 10 cm up, 5 cm right, 8 cm down, and 5 cm left.

06.1 Calculate the total distance travelled by the car. [1 mark]

_____

_____

06.2 Calculate the final displacement of the car. [3 marks]

_____

_____

_____

07.1 Describe how to find the centre of mass of a suspended piece of card. [4 marks]

_____

_____

_____

_____

_____

_____

_____

_____

HINT There are four marks for this question, so put four bullet points on the lines and try to write four separate points.

07.2 A child sits on a swing made from an old tyre (**Figure 2**). Write down what you know about the position of the centre of mass of the child and swing. [1 mark]

Figure 2

_____

_____

P8 Checklist

	Student Book	☺	😐	☹
I can write down what displacement is.	8.1			
I can write down what a vector quantity is.	8.1			
I can write down what a scalar quantity is.	8.1			
I can describe how to represent a vector quantity.	8.1			
I can write down what forces can do.	8.2			
I can write down the unit of force.	8.2			
I can write down what a contact force is.	8.2			
I can describe the forces being exerted when two objects interact.	8.2			
I can describe what a resultant force is.	8.3			
I can describe what happens if the resultant force on an object is zero.	8.3			
I can describe what happens if the resultant force on an object is greater than zero.	8.3			
I can calculate the resultant force when an object is acted on by two forces acting along the same line.	8.3			
I can write down what the centre of mass of an object is.	8.4			
I can write down where the centre of mass of a metre ruler is.	8.4			
I can find the centre of mass of an object suspended from a fixed point.	8.4			
I can find the centre of mass of a symmetrical object.	8.4			

P9.1 Speed and distance–time graphs

A If something is moving at a constant speed, you can make calculations about its motion.

Circle the letter for the correct definition of speed when the speed is constant.

X Speed is the time it takes you to travel 1 m.

Y Speed is the distance travelled divided by the time taken to travel that distance.

Z Speed is the time taken to travel a certain distance divided by the distance.

B A distance–time graph describes a journey.

Draw a line to match each sentence start to the correct ending to describe what you can work out from a distance–time graph.

If the line on the graph is horizontal		the object is travelling at high speed.

If the line on the graph is straight and steep		the object is travelling at low speed.

If the line on the graph is straight and not very steep		the object is stationary.

C An ice skater glides at a steady speed across the ice and travels a distance of 10 m in 2.5 s.

Complete the calculation to find his speed.

$$\text{speed (m/s)} = \frac{\text{distance travelled (m)}}{\text{time taken (s)}}$$

$$= \frac{\underline{\hspace{2cm}} \text{ m}}{\underline{\hspace{2cm}} \text{ s}}$$

$$= \underline{\hspace{2cm}} \text{ m/s}$$

D A skateboarder travels at 5 m/s.

Complete the calculations to answer the questions.

a How far would he travel in 10 s?

$$\text{distance travelled (m)} = \text{speed (m/s)} \times \text{time taken (s)}$$

$$= \underline{\hspace{2cm}} \text{ m/s} \times \underline{\hspace{2cm}} \text{ s}$$

$$= \underline{\hspace{2cm}} \text{ m}$$

b How long would it take him to travel 200 m?

$$\text{time taken (s)} = \frac{\text{distance travelled (m)}}{\text{speed (m/s)}}$$

$$= \frac{\underline{\hspace{2cm}} \text{ m}}{\underline{\hspace{2cm}} \text{ m/s}}$$

$$= \underline{\hspace{2cm}} \text{ s}$$

What you need to remember

You can calculate speed using this equation, with units in the brackets:

$$\text{speed } (\underline{\hspace{1cm}}) = \frac{\underline{\hspace{2cm}} (\underline{\hspace{1cm}})}{\underline{\hspace{2cm}} (\underline{\hspace{1cm}})}$$

[You need to remember this equation.]

The distance–time graph for a _____ object is a horizontal straight line, and the distance–time

graph for an object moving with a _____ _____ is a straight line that slopes upwards.

The _____ of a distance-time graph for an object tells you the object's speed.

P9.2 Velocity and acceleration

A Complete the table by ticking the boxes to show whether each statement is true for a vector quantity or a scalar quantity, or tick both boxes if it is true for both.

Statement	✓ if true for scalar quantity	✓ if true for vector quantity
This has direction.		
This has magnitude.		

B Circle the vectors in the list below.

10 m/s north   25 mph   38 mph south   10 m/s   38 mph

C The velocity of a scooter changes from 2 m/s to 5 m/s over 10 seconds.

Complete the calculation to find the acceleration.

$$\text{acceleration (m/s}^2) = \frac{\text{change in velocity (m/s)}}{\text{time taken for the change (s)}}$$

change in velocity = _____ m/s – _____ m/s

= _____ m/s

acceleration = _____ m/s

_____ s

= _____ ____

D We often write *u* for the initial speed and *v* for the final speed.

Tick the box for each situation below to show whether the object is speeding up or slowing down.

u in m/s	*v* in m/s	✓ if accelerating	✓ if decelerating
0	20		
8	20		
4	2		

What you need to remember

Velocity is the speed in a given _____ .

A _____ quantity is a physical quantity that has magnitude and direction. A _____ quantity is a physical quantity that has magnitude only.

You can calculate acceleration using this equation, with units in the brackets:

$$\text{acceleration (\_\_\_\_)} = \frac{(\_\_\_\_\_)}{(\_\_\_\_\_)}$$

[You need to remember this equation.]

Deceleration is the change of velocity per second when an object _____ _____ .

P9.3 More about velocity–time graphs

A Write a sentence to describe **one** practical method of producing a velocity–time graph.

_____

_____

B You produce a graph using the method in activity **A**.

Circle the correct **bold** words and phrases from the sentences below.

If the line on a velocity–time graph slopes up, this means that the acceleration is **negative/positive**, and the object is **slowing down/speeding up**. If the line slopes down, this means that the acceleration is **negative/positive**, and the object is **slowing down/speeding up**.

A horizontal line means that the velocity of the object **is/is not** changing.

C Here is a velocity–time graph for an object moving with constant acceleration.

Use the graph to complete the sentences below.

The final velocity of the object is _____ m/s, and the initial velocity is _____ m/s. The velocity changes over a

time of _____ s, so the acceleration is _____ m/s^2.

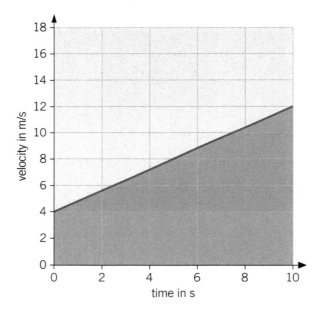

What you need to remember

You can use a _____ _____ linked to a computer to measure velocity changes.

The _____ of the line on a velocity-time graph tells you the acceleration. If the line is horizontal the

acceleration is _____ .

If the object has a positive acceleration the line has a positive _____ .

If the object is decelerating the line has a _____ gradient.

P9.4 Analysing motion graphs

A An object travels a distance of 20 m in 10 s at a steady speed, and is then stationary for 10 s. Then its speed steadily increases for 10 s.

Draw lines to match the starts and endings to make **three** correct sentences.

The speed in the first 10 s	is the gradient of the graph at that time.

The speed in the second 10 s	is 2 m/s.

The speed at any time in the last 10 s	is zero.

B Here is the velocity–time graph for a train travelling between two stations.

Tick the correct statements based on the information in the graph.

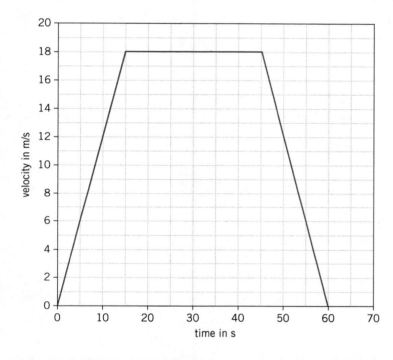

Statement	✓ if correct
The magnitude of the acceleration is the same as the magnitude of the deceleration.	
The train is stationary for 30 minutes.	
The train travels at a steady speed for 30 minutes.	

> ## What you need to remember
>
> You can find the speed from a distance–time graph by finding the _____ of the line on the graph .
>
> You can find the acceleration from a velocity–time graph by finding the _____ of the line on the graph.

P9 Practice questions

01 A ball rolls along the ground at a steady speed, and travels 1 m in 2.5 s.

Circle the correct method for calculating the speed. [1 mark]

$$\text{speed} = 1\,\text{m} \times 2.5\,\text{s} \qquad \text{speed} = \frac{2.5\,\text{s}}{1\,\text{m}}$$

$$\text{speed} = \frac{1\,\text{m}}{2.5\,\text{s}} \qquad \text{speed} = 1\,\text{m} + 2.5\,\text{s}$$

02 Describe the difference between a vector quantity and a scalar quantity. [1 mark]

03 Complete **Table 1** by calculating speed, distance, or time. [3 marks]

Table 1

Steady speed in m/s	Distance in m	Time in s
	5	5
10		2
100	300	

04 Riya drops her phone. It accelerates from a vertical speed of 0 m/s to a speed of 0.5 m/s in a time of 0.05 s. Calculate the acceleration. [3 marks]

05 **Figure 1** is a graph showing a person's journey.

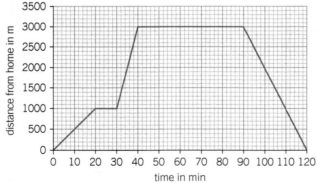

Figure 1

05.1 Write down **one** of the distances from home at which the person was stationary. [1 mark]

05.2 Write down the times between which the person was walking fastest. [1 mark]

05.3 Explain why you could label the y-axis 'displacement'. [1 mark]

06 **Figure 2** shows the velocity–time graph for a cyclist.

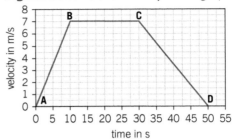

Figure 2

Describe the motion of the cyclist:

06.1 between points **A** and **B** [2 marks]

06.2 between points **B** and **C** [1 mark]

06.3 between points **C** and **D**. [2 marks]

07 Write down or calculate the acceleration of the cyclist in **Figure 2**:

07.1 between points **A** and **B** [2 marks]

07.2 between points **B** and **C**. [1 mark]

08 Compare section **A** to **B** and section **C** to **D** on the graph in **Figure 2**.

08.1 Circle the word or phrase that compares the acceleration between **C** and **D** with the acceleration between **A** and **B**. [1 mark]

double   **the same**   **half**

08.2 Explain your answer. [2 marks]

P9 Checklist

	Student Book	☺	☻	☹
I can calculate the speed of an object moving at constant speed.	9.1			
I can use a distance–time graph to determine whether an object is stationary or moving at constant speed.	9.1			
I can write down what the gradient of the line on a distance–time graph can tell you.	9.1			
I can use the equation for constant speed to calculate distance moved or time taken.	9.1			
I can write down the difference between speed and velocity.	9.2			
I can calculate the acceleration of an object.	9.2			
I can write down the difference between acceleration and deceleration.	9.2			
I can measure velocity change.	9.3			
I can write down what a horizontal line on a velocity–time graph tells you.	9.3			
I can use a velocity–time graph.	9.3			
I can work out whether an object is accelerating or decelerating.	9.3			
I can calculate acceleration from a velocity–time graph.	9.4			

P10.1 Forces and acceleration

A The force on an moving object, its mass, and its acceleration are linked.

Complete the table by writing 'increases' or 'decreases' in each empty box.

If the force...	...and the mass...	...then the acceleration...
increases	stays the same	
decreases	stays the same	
stays the same	increases	
stays the same	decreases	

B Use the words and phrases below to complete the sentences about forces and acceleration. You will need to use one of the words or phrases twice.

doubles   **halves**   **stays the same**   **proportional**   **inversely proportional**

The acceleration of an object is _____ to the force on the object.

So if the force doubles, the acceleration _____ , as long as the mass _____ _____ _____ .

The acceleration of an object is _____ to the mass of the object. So if the mass doubles,

the acceleration _____ , as long as the force _____ _____ _____ .

C A ball has a mass of 100 g. It has an acceleration of 3 m/s².

Complete the calculation to find the the force on the ball.

resultant force (N) = mass (kg) × acceleration (m/s²)

mass = 100 g = _____ kg

resultant force = _____ kg × _____ m/s²

= _____ N

What you need to remember

If the resultant force on an object increases, the acceleration will _____ , as long as the _____ stays the same.

If two objects of different masses have the same resultant force acting on them, the acceleration of the object with the bigger mass will be _____ .

You can calculate the resultant force acting on an object using this equation, with units in the brackets:

resultant force (_____) = _____ (_____) × _____ (_____)

[You need to remember this equation.]

P10.2 Weight and terminal velocity

A A falling object on Earth accelerates because of the force of gravity acting on it.

Circle the order of magnitude value of the acceleration of an object, in m/s², if the only force acting on it is gravity.

0.01	0.1	1	10	100	1000

B People often confuse weight and mass.

Tick the **two** statements that correctly describe what weight and mass are.

Statement	✓ if correct
Mass is the quantity of matter in an object.	
Weight is the same as mass but in a different unit.	
Mass is your weight in kilograms.	
Weight is the force of gravity acting on an object.	

C Complete the table with the correct values of mass and weight.

Mass in kg	Gravitational field strength in N/kg	Weight in N
1	9.8	
	9.8	30
10	1.6	

D Sort these statements in order to describe and explain what happens when you drop a tennis ball and it falls through the air.

Write the letters in the correct order below.

W As it accelerates the frictional force acting on it increases.

X When the forces acting on the ball are equal and opposite, the ball falls with terminal velocity.

Y When you first drop the ball, it accelerates.

Z Eventually the frictional force equals the weight.

Correct order: _____

What you need to remember

The weight of an object is the _____ acting on the object due to gravity. The mass is the quantity of _____ in the object.

If there is only gravity acting on an object, then it will accelerate at about _____ m/s².

When an object falls, it eventually reaches _____ velocity. This happens when the weight equals the _____ force on the object. At this velocity, the resultant force on the object is _____ .

P10.3 Forces and braking

A Driving too quickly is dangerous because it takes longer to stop the car.

Draw a line to match each start to the correct ending to make **three** sentences about the distances involved when a vehicle stops.

Braking distance is	the thinking distance plus the braking distance.
Thinking distance is	the distance that the car travels when the brakes are on.
Stopping distance is	the distance that the car travels while the driver reacts.

B Do the factors in the table affect thinking distance, stopping distance, or both?

Write 'yes' or 'no' in each box.

Factor	Does it affect thinking distance?	Does it affect braking distance?
snow / ice on the road		
being tired		
speed		
drinking alcohol		
using a phone		

C A car of mass 1000 kg is braking. Its deceleration is 4 m/s².

Complete the calculation to find the force exerted by the brakes, then convert your answer to kN.

force (N) = mass (kg) × acceleration (m/s²)

= _____ kg × _____ m/s²

= _____ N = _____ kN

What you need to remember

Friction and air resistance oppose the _____ force of a vehicle.

The stopping distance of a vehicle depends on the _____ distance and the _____ distance.

Poor weather conditions, poor vehicle maintenance, and speed affect the _____ distance. Poor reaction time and high speed both affect the _____ distance.

You can work out the braking force of a vehicle using this equation, with units in the brackets:

force (_____) = _____ (_____) × _____ (_____)

[You need to remember this equation.]

P10.5 Forces and elasticity

A Some materials behave in a way that is described as **elastic**.

Circle the letter to show the correct definition of elastic.

W Something that stretches is elastic.

X Something that needs a large force to stretch it is elastic.

Y Something that does not return to its original shape when you remove the force is elastic.

Z Something that does return to its original shape when you remove the force
is elastic.

B Hooke's law links the extension of a spring to the force applied to it.

A student has a spring with a spring constant of 40 N/m. The spring is 3.0 cm long to start with. It is 4.5 cm long when she applies a force.

Complete the calculation to find the extension and the force.

force applied (N) = spring constant (N/m) × extension (m)

extension = _____ cm − _____ cm

= _____ cm = _____ m

force = _____ N/m × _____ m

= _____ N

C If you hang different weights on a spring, a graph like the one below tells you about the relationship between the extension and the weight.

Fill in the gaps to complete the sentences.

For this spring, the relationship is linear below a force of _____ N.

You know this because the line on the graph is a _____ line. The

extension is _____ _____ to the force.

Above this force, the relationship is _____ - _____ , and the line on

the graph is a _____ .

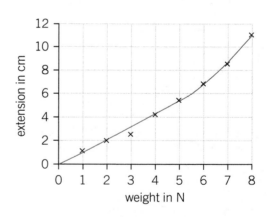

What you need to remember

An object is _____ if it returns to its original shape after you remove the force that you have used
to deform it.

The extension of an object is the _____ between the length when you stretch it and its original
length.

The extension of a spring is _____ _____ to the force applied to it. This is only true if you
do *not* go beyond the limit of _____ . This is a _____ relationship.

If you *do* go beyond the limit of _____ , then the relationship becomes _____ – _____ ,
and the force and extension are no longer _____ .

P10 Practice questions

01 Circle the **two** quantities that you need to know if you want to calculate the acceleration of an object.

[2 marks]

speed   time   mass   velocity   force

02 Draw lines to link the boxes below to make **three** correct sentences about force, mass, and acceleration. You must use each box once.

[2 marks]

If the force on a trolley increases	and the force stays the same,	the acceleration decreases.
If the mass of a trolley increases	and the mass stays the same,	the acceleration increases.
If you double the force	and you double the mass,	the acceleration stays the same.

03.1 Write down **one** factor that affects the braking distance of a car.

[1 mark]

_____

_____

03.2 Write down **one** factor that will increase the reaction time of a car driver.

[1 mark]

_____

_____

04 Complete **Table 1** by calculating the resultant force.

[3 marks]

Table 1

Mass in kg	Acceleration in m/s²	Resultant force in N
1	2	
0.5	2	
100	0.02	

05 You want to measure the extension of a spring and calculate the spring constant. Circle the correct **bold** words to complete the sentences.

05.1 To calculate the extension of a spring, you

add/subtract the original length from the

extended length.

[1 mark]

05.2 To calculate the spring constant, you

divide/multiply the force by the extension.

[1 mark]

05.3 **Figure 1** shows a graph of extension against weight for a stretched spring.

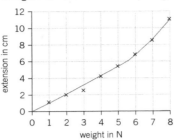

Figure 1

Write down the value of the limit of proportionality.

[1 mark]

_____

05.4 Use measurements shown in **Figure 1** to calculate the spring constant.

[4 marks]

_____

_____

06 You drop a ping-pong ball. One of the forces acting on the ball is the force of the Earth on the ball.

06.1 Write down the other force acting on the ball as it falls.

[1 mark]

_____

06.2 Kyle uses a motion sensor to collect data about the speed of the ball as it falls. **Table 2** shows his results.

Table 2

Time in s	Speed in m/s
0.0	0
0.1	1
0.2	2
0.3	3
0.4	3
0.5	3

Write down the value of the terminal velocity.

_____ [1 mark]

06.3 Describe and explain the motion of the object between 0 s and 0.3 s. [3 marks]

HINT Remember, resultant forces change speeds.

_____

_____

_____

06.4 Describe and explain the motion of the object between 0.3 s and 0.5 s. [3 marks]

_____

_____

_____

P10 Checklist

	Student Book	😊	😐	😞
I can describe how the acceleration of an object depends on the size of the resultant force acting upon it.	10.1			
I can describe the effect that the mass of an object has on its acceleration.	10.1			
I can describe how to calculate the resultant force on an object from its acceleration and its mass.	10.1			
I can describe the difference between mass and weight.	10.2			
I can describe and explain the motion of a falling object acted on only by gravity.	10.2			
I can write down what terminal velocity means.	10.2			
I can write down what can be said about the resultant force acting on an object that is falling at terminal velocity.	10.2			
I can describe the forces that oppose the driving force of a vehicle.	10.3			
I can write down what the stopping distance of a vehicle depends on.	10.3			
I can write down what can increase the stopping distance of a vehicle.	10.3			
I can estimate the braking force of a vehicle.	10.3			
I can write down what 'elastic' means.	10.5			
I can describe how to measure the extension of an object when it is stretched.	10.5			
I can describe how the extension of a spring changes with the force applied to it.	10.5			
I can write down what the limit of proportionality of a spring means.	10.5			

P11.1 The nature of waves

A There are many different types of wave. What do waves transfer?

Circle the **two** correct words.

energy   matter   water   air   information   light

B Waves are either **transverse** or **longitudinal**.

Tick the boxes to show whether each statement is true for transverse waves or longitudinal waves.

Statements	✓ if true for transverse waves	✓ if true for longitudinal waves
Oscillations are in the same direction as the energy transfer.		
Oscillations are perpendicular to the direction of energy transfer.		
Sound waves are an example.		
Electromagnetic waves are an example.		

C Circle the correct **bold** words and phrases to complete these sentences about waves.

Sound needs a medium to travel through, so it is **an electromagnetic/a mechanical** wave. When a tuning fork vibrates it pushes the air, producing **compressions/rarefactions**, and pulls the air, producing **compressions/rarefactions**.

A wave that needs air, water, or the ground to travel through is **an electromagnetic/a mechanical** wave.

All **electromagnetic/mechanical** waves are transverse waves.

You **can/cannot** make transverse *and* longitudinal waves on a long spring. You **can/cannot** make transverse *and* longitudinal waves on a rope.

What you need to remember

You can use waves to transfer _____ and energy.

A wave that oscillates perpendicular (at 90°) to the direction of energy transfer is called a

_____ wave. Examples of these waves are the _____ on the

surface of water, and _____ waves, such as light.

A wave that oscillates parallel to the direction of energy transfer is called a _____ wave.

An example of this kind of wave is a _____ wave produced by a loudspeaker.

Mechanical waves need a _____ to travel through.

P11.2 The properties of waves

A Tick the **three** statements about the properties of electromagnetic waves that are correct.

	Statement	✓ if correct
P	The distance from one peak to the next peak is the wavelength.	
Q	Frequency is the number of waves per second.	
R	The unit of frequency is seconds.	
S	The unit of wavelength is metres.	
T	The distance from a peak to a trough is the amplitude.	

Write corrected versions of the **two** statements that are incorrect.

_____

_____

_____

_____

B A musical instrument makes a note with a frequency of 660 Hz, and a wavelength of 0.5m.

Complete the calculations to find the period and wavelength of the sound wave.

a period (_____) = $\dfrac{1}{\text{frequency (_____)}}$

$= \dfrac{1}{\text{_____ Hz}}$

$= $ _____ s

b wave speed (m/s) = frequency (Hz) × wavelength (m)

$= $ _____ Hz × _____ m

$= $ _____ m/s

What you need to remember

The amplitude of a wave is the _____ displacement of a point on the wave from its undisturbed position. This could be the height of a wave _____, or the height of a wave _____ .

The wavelength of a wave is the distance from a point on a wave to the _____ point on the next wave. This could be from one wave _____ to the next wave crest.

You can calculate the period of a wave using this equation, with units in the brackets:

period (_____) = $\dfrac{1}{\text{_____ (_____)}}$

[You need to remember this equation.]

You can calculate the speed of a wave using this equation, with units in the brackets:

speed (_____) = _____ (_____) × _____ (_____)

[You need to remember this equation.]

P11.4 More about waves

A Circle the letter for the correct definition of an **echo**.

P   An echo is a refraction of sound.

Q   An echo is the spreading out of sound from a source.

R   An echo is a reflection of sound.

S   An echo is the size of a sound wave.

B Sort these statements in order to describe how you measure the speed of sound.

Write the letters in the correct order below.

V   Make a short loud sound.

W   Measure a long distance from a large building and stand that distance away.

X   Multiply the distance by 2 and note this distance to use in your calculations after the experiment.

Y   Measure the time to hear the echo of the sound.

Z   Use the equation speed = distance/time to calculate the speed.

Correct order: _____

C Aran carried out the experiment described in activity **B**. He stood a distance of 150 m from a wall and measured a time delay of 0.9 s between making the sound and hearing the echo.

Complete the calculation to find the speed of sound. (Use 2 significant figures in your answer.)

$$\text{speed (m/s)} = \frac{\text{total distance (m)}}{\text{time (s)}}$$

total distance travelled by the sound = 2 × distance to wall = 2 × _____ m

= _____ m

$$\text{speed} = \frac{_____ \text{ m}}{_____ \text{ s}}$$

= _____ m/s = _____ m/s to 2 significant figures

What you need to remember

You hear an echo when a sound wave _____ from a smooth, hard surface.

You can measure the speed of sound by measuring the _____ interval between seeing a short loud sound being made and hearing it. If you also measure the _____ you can use the equation:

$$\text{speed (\_\_\_\_)} = \frac{_____ (\_\_\_\_)}{_____ (\_\_\_\_)}$$

to find the speed of sound.

P11 Practice questions

01 Tick the boxes by the correct definitions below.

[2 marks]

The period of the wave is the time for one whole wave. ☐

The frequency is the number of waves. ☐

The period is the time of a wave. ☐

The frequency is the number of waves per second. ☐

02 Look at **Figure 1** and complete **Table 1** by writing the correct letter or letters in the boxes. There are two letters you do not need to use. [4 marks]

Figure 1

Table 1

Wave property	Letter or letters
wavelength	
amplitude	

03 Draw a line to match each type of wave to its correct description and example. [2 marks]

Types of wave	Descriptions	Examples
A mechanical wave	does not need a medium to travel through,	such as light.
An electromagnetic wave	does need a medium to travel through,	such as sound.

04 Use these words or phrases to complete the sentences below.

perpendicular to   **in the same direction as**

compressions   **rarefactions**

04.1 In a longitudinal wave, the oscillations are _____ the direction of energy transfer. [1 mark]

04.2 In a transverse wave the oscillations are _____ the direction of energy transfer. [1 mark]

04.3 As a sound wave travels through the air, there are regions where the air is squashed, called _____ , and regions where it is stretched, called _____ . [2 marks]

05 A sound wave underwater has a frequency of 1000 Hz and a wavelength of 1.5 m.

05.1 Calculate the speed of sound in water. [3 marks]

_____

_____

_____

05.2 Calculate the period of the wave. [3 marks]

_____

_____

_____

06 A group of students carried out an experiment to measure the speed of sound. They stood a long way from a wall and made a sound. Here are their results.

distance to wall = 200 m, time = 1.3 s

06.1 Suggest **two** measuring instruments that they used to make these measurements. [2 marks]

_____

_____

06.2 Describe how they measured the time in this experiment. [2 marks]

_____

_____

06.3 Use the data to calculate the speed of sound. Write your answer to 2 significant figures.

[4 marks]

_____

_____

_____

_____

06.4 Write down **one** improvement that the students could make to their experiment based on the data. [1 mark]

HINT Think about how you obtain accurate results.

_____

_____

_____

_____

P11 Checklist

	Student Book	☺	☺	☹
I can describe what waves can be used for.	11.1			
I can describe what transverse waves are.	11.1			
I can write down what longitudinal waves are.	11.1			
I can write down which types of wave are transverse and which are longitudinal.	11.1			
I can define the amplitude, frequency, and wavelength of a wave mean.	11.2			
I can describe how the period of a wave is related to its frequency.	11.2			
I can write down the relationship between the speed, wavelength, and frequency of a wave.	11.2			
I can use the wave speed equation in calculations.	11.2			
I can write down what sound waves are.	11.4			
I can write down what echoes are.	11.4			
I can describe how to measure the speed of sound in air.	11.4			

A Waves from different parts of the electromagnetic spectrum have different wavelengths and frequencies. This diagram shows the waves of the electromagnetic spectrum.

a Fill in the missing waves.

radio			visible			gamma

b Which wave has the biggest wavelength? Colour the box blue.
c Which wave has the biggest frequency? Colour the box red.
d Which wave has the biggest energy? Outline the box in green.
e Which wave can our eyes detect? Outline the box in yellow.

B Write a sentence to describe in terms of energy what electromagnetic waves do.

_____

_____

C **a** Circle in blue the smallest wavelength that our eyes can detect.
b Circle in red the largest wavelength that our eyes can detect.

| 250 nm | 300 nm | 350 nm | 400 nm | 450 nm | 500 nm |

| 550 nm | 600 nm | 650 nm | 700 nm | 750 nm |

D The wavelength of microwaves is 3 cm and their frequency is 10 000 000 000 Hz.

Complete the calculation to find the speed of microwaves.
wave speed (m/s) = frequency (Hz) × wavelength (m)

wavelength = _____ cm = _____ m

wave speed = _____ Hz × _____ m

= _____ m/s

What you need to remember

The waves of the electromagnetic spectrum are:

radio, _____ , _____ , _____ light, _____ , _____ - _____ , and gamma rays.

This list of waves is in order from the _____ to the _____ wavelength, and from the _____ to the _____ frequency and energy.

The human eye can only detect _____ light, which has a range of wavelengths from _____ nm to _____ nm.

Electromagnetic waves transfer energy from a _____ to an _____ .

You can use the wave equation:

wave _____ (___) = _____ (___) × _____ (___)

to calculate the frequency and wavelength of electromagnetic waves.

[You need to remember this equation.]

P12.2 Light, infrared, microwaves, and radio waves

A Light from the Sun is called white light.

Complete the sentences by circling the correct **bold** words.

You can use a glass **block/prism** to split visible light into the colours of the visible **species/spectrum**. Light can produce an **image/shadow** on photographic film, or using a sensor containing pixels in a **digital/portable** camera.

B All these devices use infrared radiation.

Tick the boxes to show how each device uses infrared.

Device	✓ if it detects infrared	✓ if it emits infrared	✓ if infrared transfers information
infrared scanner in medicine			
remote control			
infrared camera			
electric heater			

C Circle the letter of the correct statement about microwaves.

W Microwaves heat the inside of a microwave oven, and this cooks the food.

X Microwaves cannot heat anything that contains water.

Y Microwave ovens cannot heat food as quickly as ordinary ovens.

Z Microwaves are absorbed by the water molecules in food and this heats the food.

D Draw a line to link the starts and endings to make **three** correct sentences about radio waves and microwaves.

We use microwaves for satellite TV	because they heat up parts of the body.
Microwaves and radio waves can be hazardous	because they transmit information without wires.
We use radio waves for connecting computers to other devices	because they can pass through the atmosphere.

What you need to remember

White light contains all the _____ of the visible spectrum.

Infrared radiation is used to carry _____ from remote control handsets and inside _____ fibres.

Your mobile phone uses _____ waves and _____ . Satellite TV uses _____ , and radio and TV broadcasting uses _____ _____ .

Different types of electromagnetic radiation are hazardous in different ways. _____ waves and _____ can heat parts of the body, and _____ radiation can cause skin burns.

P12.3 Communications

A Sort the uses of radio waves and microwaves in order of those that need the shortest wavelength to those that need the longest wavelength.

Write the letters in the correct order below.

W local radio stations

X satellite TV and satellite phones

Y international radio stations

Z TV broadcasting

Correct order: _____

B These statements are about the hazards of mobile phone radiation.

Tick the box of the statement that is true.

P Mobile phone radiation is safe because many people use their phones ☐
without having a problem.

Q Mobile phones use microwaves. These heat your brain which is ☐
definitely harmful.

R Mobile phone radiation has the same effect on children and adults. ☐

S Mobile phone radiation may be dangerous, but scientists need to do ☐
more research to find out.

C Circle the correct **bold** words to explain the uses of waves in communication.

We use radio waves with a short wavelength to send information over **long/short** distances because they have a **bigger/smaller** range. Waves with a shorter wavelength spread out **less/more**. Waves with a shorter wavelength are absorbed **less/more** by the atmosphere.

Optical fibres carry **less/more** information than radio waves or microwaves because the light sent down them has a much **longer/shorter** wavelength. Information sent down optical fibres is secure because the light is **reflected/ refracted** back into the fibre so it does not escape.

What you need to remember

We use radio waves of different frequencies for different purposes. This is because the wavelength and frequency affect the _____ they travel, how much they _____ out, and how much _____ they can carry.

We use _____ to transmit satellite TV signals.

We need further _____ before we will know whether or not mobile phones are safe to use.

We send signals by _____ or _____ radiation down thin transparent fibres called optical fibres.

A Tick the boxes to show whether each statement about ultraviolet waves is true or false.

Statement	✓ if true	✓ if false
Ultraviolet waves lie between X-rays and gamma rays in the electromagnetic spectrum.		
Ultraviolet waves can cause lung cancer.		
Ultraviolet waves can cause skin cancer.		
Ultraviolet waves have a longer wavelength than visible light.		

B Circle the letters for the **two** properties of gamma rays that are very different from those of X-rays.

W their wavelength

X how they are produced

Y their position in the electromagnetic spectrum

Z their penetrating power

C Sort these statements in order to explain how cancer forms in the human body.

Write the letters in the correct order below.

P As it passes through, the X-ray or gamma ray knocks an electron out of an atom.

Q Ionisation can kill the cell or damage the DNA of the cell.

R An X-ray or a gamma ray passes through human tissue.

S This process is called ionisation.

T Damaged DNA can cause cancer.

Correct order: _____

What you need to remember

Ultraviolet waves have a _____ wavelength than visible light, and can harm the

_____ and eyes.

X-rays are used by doctors in _____ to make X-ray images.

Gamma rays are used to kill harmful _____ in food, to _____ surgical

equipment, and to kill _____ cells.

When _____ radiation travels through matter, it can make uncharged atoms charged.

X-rays and gamma rays can cause _____ to living tissue when they pass through it.

P12.5 X-rays in medicine

A Here are some uses of X-rays and gamma rays.

Tick the boxes to show which uses are true for X-rays and for gamma rays.

Use	✓ if true for X-rays	✓ if true for gamma rays
producing images of broken limbs		
killing cancer cells inside the body		
killing skin cancer cells		

B Sort these statements in order to explain how a dentist takes an X-ray of a tooth to find tooth decay.

Write the letters in the correct order below.

P Position an X-ray machine so that the X-rays can pass through the tooth to the detector.

Q Turn on the X-ray machine.

R Place the patient in front of a piece of photographic film or a CCD detector.

S Put lead screening in front of any parts of the person that do not need imaging, and leave the room if you are operating the machine.

T Look for a dark area on the image of the tooth, which shows a hole.

U Develop the film, or process the image with a computer.

Correct order: _____

C Write a sentence to explain why X-rays are dangerous.

_____

_____

D **a** Circle the material that absorbs X-rays the most.

b Draw a box around the material that absorbs X-rays the least.

thin metal   **skin**   **thick metal**   **bone**

What you need to remember

X-rays are used in hospitals to make X-ray images and to destroy _____ cells at or near the body surface.

X-rays are _____ radiation, so they can damage living tissue when they pass through it.

Bones and teeth _____ more X-rays passing through the body than soft tissue does.

P12 Practice questions

01 Here are the waves of the electromagnetic spectrum. There is a letter for each wave. They are not in order.

A	B	C	D	E	F	G
infrared radiation	radio waves	gamma rays	microwaves	X-rays	visible light	ultraviolet radiation

01.1 Write the letter of the wave with the biggest

frequency. _____ [1 mark]

01.2 Write the letter of the wave our eyes can detect.

_____ [1 mark]

01.3 Write the letters or names of the waves in order, starting with the wave with the biggest wavelength. [6 marks]

_____

02 **Figure 1** shows an optical fibre.

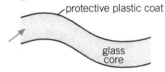

Figure 1

02.1 Write down **one** type of electromagnetic radiation that travels down an optical fibre. [1 mark]

_____

02.2 Complete the diagram to show how the radiation travels down the fibre. [2 marks]

03 Complete the following four sentences using the labels below. You need to use one of the labels in the first row twice.

emits   emits and absorbs   absorbs

radio waves   microwaves   infrared

radiation   visible light

A mobile phone _____ _____.

A TV aerial _____ _____.

A remote control _____ _____.

Photographic film _____ _____.

04 Choose from the **bold** words below to complete the sentences. [3 marks]

long   short   ground   atmosphere   spread

You need to use waves with a _____ wavelength to transmit information through the _____ to satellites. This is because the waves do not _____ out very much.

05 Look at **Figure 2**, which was produced in a hospital.

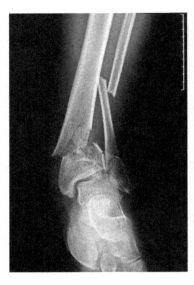

Figure 2

05.1 Write down the type of electromagnetic radiation used to produce this image. [1 mark]

_____

05.2 Explain why some parts of the image are black, and some are white. [3 marks]

_____

_____

_____

05.3 This radiation is ionising. Describe what 'ionising' means. [1 mark]

_____

05.4 Name **one** other wave of the electromagnetic spectrum that is ionising. [1 mark]

_____

05.5 Describe **one** precaution that the person making this image should take to reduce the risk of injury. [1 mark]

_____

_____

06 The frequency of a radio wave is 100 000 000 Hz, and it travels at 300 000 000 m/s. Calculate the wavelength of the radio wave. [3 marks]

HINT Remember, speed = frequency × wavelength

_____

_____

_____

P12 Checklist

	Student Book	☺	😐	☹
I can write down the parts of the electromagnetic spectrum.	12.1			
I can write down the range of wavelengths within the electromagnetic spectrum that the human eye can detect.	12.1			
I can describe how energy is transferred by electromagnetic waves.	12.1			
I can calculate the frequency or wavelength of electromagnetic waves.	12.1			
I can describe the nature of white light.	12.2			
I can name some uses of infrared radiation, microwaves, and radio waves.	12.2			
I can write down what mobile phone radiation is.	12.2			
I can explain why these types of electromagnetic radiation are hazardous.	12.2			
I can explain why radio waves of different frequencies are used for different purposes.	12.3			
I can write down which waves are used for satellite TV.	12.3			
I can describe how to decide whether or not mobile phones are safe to use.	12.3			
I can describe how optical fibres are used in communications.	12.3			
I can describe the differences between ultraviolet and visible light.	12.4			
I can name some uses of X-rays and gamma rays.	12.4			
I can write down what ionising radiation is.	12.4			
I can explain why ultraviolet waves, X-rays, and gamma rays are dangerous.	12.4			
I can describe what X-rays are used for in hospitals.	12.5			
I can explain why X-rays are dangerous.	12.5			
I can write down which parts absorb X-rays when they pass through the body.	12.5			

P13.1 Magnetic fields

A A pole of one magnet may attract or repel a pole of another magnet.

Complete the last column of the table to describe what happens when you bring two magnets, **P** and **Q**, together.

Pole on P		Pole on Q	The magnets will....
north	...brought together with...	north	
north	...brought together with...	south	
south	...brought together with...	north	
south	...brought together with...	south	

B Complete the diagram by adding arrows to the magnetic field lines to show the direction of the magnetic field.

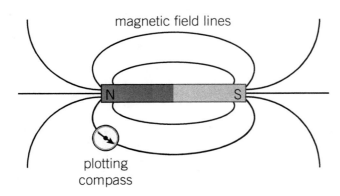

magnetic field lines

N   S

plotting
compass

C Draw lines to link the starts and endings to make **three** correct sentences about magnets and induced magnets.

If you put a piece of magnetic material in a magnetic field,	it will become magnetic but will lose its magnetism easily.

If you put iron in a magnetic field,	it will become an induced magnet.

If you put steel in a magnetic field,	it will become magnetic and will not lose its magnetism easily.

What you need to remember

When you bring two magnet poles together, they will _____ if the poles are the same, and

_____ if the poles are different.

The magnetic field lines of a bar magnet are in a direction from the _____ pole of the magnet

to the _____ pole of the magnet.

If you put a piece of magnetic material in a magnetic field, it will become an _____ magnet.

Permanent magnets are made out of _____ because it does not lose its magnetism easily.

A magnetic material such as _____ does lose its magnetism easily.

A Complete the diagram to show the shape and direction of the magnetic field around a current-carrying wire. The current in the wire is in a direction into the paper.

B We model magnetic fields using field lines.

Draw lines to link the boxes to make **three** correct statements about magnetic field lines.

Parallel magnetic field lines show that	the magnetic field is getting stronger,	or the force on a magnetic material.
Magnetic field lines that are getting closer together show that	the direction of the field	such as near the end of a solenoid.
The direction of the arrow on the field line shows	the field is uniform,	such as in the middle of a solenoid.

C Complete the following sentences about the magnetic field around a current-carrying wire.

If you reverse the direction of the electric current without changing the size of the current, the magnetic field will

_____ . The distance between the field lines will stay the _____ .

If a magnetic field is weak then the field lines are _____ . If the field is strong then the field lines are

_____ .

What you need to remember

To draw the magnetic field pattern around a current-carrying wire, you need to draw _____ centred on the wire.

The magnetic field lines inside a solenoid are _____ and all in the same direction.

You can increase the strength of the magnetic field around a wire or in a solenoid by _____ the current. If you reverse the current, you _____ the direction of the magnetic field.

For a uniform magnetic field, the field lines are all _____ to each other.

P13 Practice questions

01 There is a magnetic field around some objects, but not around others.

Circle **all** the objects below that have a magnetic field around them. [2 marks]

piece of wire   bar magnet   piece of iron

wire with an electric current flowing in it

02 Write down the rule for working out what happens when you bring the poles of two magnets together. [2 marks]

_____

_____

_____

03 Tick the box next to the correct statement or statements about the magnetic field around a solenoid. [2 marks]

The magnetic field around a solenoid gets ☐
weaker as you get closer to the solenoid.

The magnetic field inside a solenoid is uniform. ☐

The magnetic field around a solenoid has the ☐
same shape as that around a bar magnet.

The larger the current in a solenoid, the ☐
weaker the field is.

04 **Figure 1** shows the magnetic field patterns around two current-carrying wires.

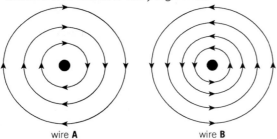

wire **A**   wire **B**

Figure 1

Use **Figure 1** to complete these sentences by circling the correct **bold** word or phrase.

04.1 The diagrams show that the current in wire **B** is

in the **opposite/same** direction as the current in

wire **A**, because the arrows on the magnetic field

lines are in the **opposite/same** direction.

[2 marks]

04.2 For both wires the diagrams show that the

magnetic field strength **decreases/increases**

as you move away from the wire, because the

distance between the field lines

decreases/increases. [2 marks]

04.3 The diagrams show that the current in wire **B** is **larger/smaller** than the current in wire **A** because the field lines for wire **B** are **closer together/further apart** than they are for wire **A**. [2 marks]

05 Some materials become magnetic when they are placed in a magnetic field.

05.1 Write down the name of this type of magnetism.

[1 mark]

_____

05.2 Circle the materials below that become magnetic when they are placed in a magnetic field. [2 marks]

iron   aluminium   zinc   copper   steel

06.1 **Table 1** shows some different solenoids. Put them in order of strength starting with the strongest, by writing the letters in order below. The first two have been done for you.

Table 1

Solenoid	Number of turns	Current in A	Core
A	40	3	air
B	40	3	iron
C	30	2	air
D	20	2	air

Correct order: (strongest) **B**, **A**, ___, ___ (weakest)

[2 marks]

HINT Find the weakest and the strongest electromagnet first.

06.2 Explain why solenoid **B** is stronger than solenoid **A**. [3 marks]

HINT Remember that magnetic materials become magnetised in a magnetic field.

_____

_____

06.3 A student can put a compass **inside** solenoids **A**, **C**, and **D**. Describe and explain what she would see if she moved the compass inside those solenoids. [2 marks]

HINT Remember that the field inside a solenoid is uniform.

_____

_____

_____

_____

P13 Checklist

	Student Book	☺	☺	☹
I can write down the force rule for two magnetic poles near each other.	13.1			
I can describe the pattern of magnetic field lines around a bar magnet.	13.1			
I can write down what induced magnetism is.	13.1			
I can explain why steel, not iron, is used to make permanent magnets.	13.1			
I can describe the pattern of the magnetic field around a straight wire carrying a current.	13.2			
I can describe the pattern of the magnetic field in and around a solenoid.	13.2			
I can describe how the strength and direction of the magnetic field varies with position and current.	13.2			
I can write down what a uniform magnetic field is.	13.2			
I can write down what an electromagnet is.	13.2			

Answers

P1.1

A   energy in a **chemical store** – food, fuels, and chemicals in batteries
energy in a **kinetic store** – a moving skateboarder
energy in a **gravitational potential energy store** – a climber at the top of Everest
energy in a **thermal store** – a hot cup of coffee

B   a   an electric current
    b   a force
    c   heating, waves

C   energy in the gravitational potential energy store at the start – *both*
energy transferred by forces – *both*
energy transferred by heating/sound – *both*
energy in the gravitational potential energy store at the end – *tennis ball*
energy in the thermal energy store at the end – *keys*

What you need to remember

store
heating, waves, electric current, a force
gravitational potential, kinetic
kinetic, surroundings, heating

P1.2

A   energy cannot be created or destroyed, just transferred between stores
B   Y
C   The maximum kinetic energy is equal to the maximum gravitational potential energy.
D   the same
    would not
    would not

What you need to remember

created, destroyed, conservation, all
closed, energy
change

P1.3

A   force, a certain distance
B   cycling to school, lifting your bag into your locker
C   10 N, 2 m, **20 J**
    30 N, 10 cm, **3 J**
    25 kN, 5 m, **125 000 J**
    20 kN, 50 mm, **1000 J**
D   work done (J) = force (N) × distance (m)
            = 15 (N) × 10 (m)
            = 150 J

What you need to remember

force, transferring
J, force (N), distance (m)
air resistance, friction, heat

P1.4

A   You go up in a lift – The energy in your gravitational potential energy store increases.
You walk downstairs – The energy in your gravitational potential energy store decreases.
You run 100 m on a flat track – The energy in your gravitational potential energy store stays the same.

B   1 kg, 10, 2 m, **20 J**
    1 kg, 1.6, 10 cm, **0.16 J**
    250 g, 27, 5 m, **34 J**
    20 g, 10, 50 mm, **0.01 J**

C   change in gravitational potential energy
    = weight (N) × change in height (m)
    = 100 N × 1 m
    = 100 J

What you need to remember

increases, decreases
work, force, less, easier
J, mass (kg), gravitational, strength (N/kg), height (m)

P1.5

A   mass, speed
B   the energy in an elastic store due to a material being stretched or compressed (which is due to the stretching or compressing of bonds between atoms/molecules)
C   kinetic energy (J)
    = 0.5 × mass (kg) × (speed (m/s))²
    = 0.5 × 0.05 (kg) × (10 (m/s))²
    = 2.5 J
D   it is stationary
E   Y

What you need to remember

mass, speed
mass (kg), speed (m/s)
work, elastic

P1.6

A   **useful energy** – energy that is transferred by a pathway that we want
wasted energy – energy that is transferred by a pathway that we do not want
dissipation – the process of energy spreading out so it is not useful

B   kinetic store when the car accelerates – *useful*
thermal store of the surroundings due to friction between the gears – *wasted*
thermal store of the brakes and surroundings due to friction when slowing down – *useful*
thermal store of the surroundings due to light from the headlights – *useful*

C   riding a bicycle – e.g., heating surroundings due to friction / air resistance

using an electric drill – e.g., heating surroundings due to friction / electric current
using an electric oven – e.g., heating surroundings due to the outside of the oven being hot

What you need to remember

want
dissipation
wasted, surroundings, hotter/warmer

P1.7

A   100%
B   A more efficient device wastes more energy than a less efficient one – *false*
A less efficient device wastes more energy than an efficient one – *true*
If you had a less efficient device, you would need more input energy to get the same output energy – *true*
C   good, decreases, decreases, bad, decreases, harder
thermal
D   efficiency = $\dfrac{\text{useful energy transfer (J)}}{\text{total energy transfer (J)}}$
         = $\dfrac{400\ \text{J}}{1000\ \text{J}}$
         = 0.4

What you need to remember

useful, (J), total, (J)
100, created
friction, heating, hotter, lubricating

P1.8

A   a   electricity, gas
    b   gas, electricity
    c   electricity
B   a   a kettle
    b   it takes less time to heat the water
C   a   X
    b   Y
    c   Y requires more energy to be supplied per minute to produce the same amount of light

What you need to remember

oil
electricity, cooking/heating, lighting, microwave
less

P1.9

A   Power is the – energy transferred – divided by – the time.
B   Powerful devices are always more efficient than less powerful devices – *false*
A less powerful device wastes more energy than an efficient one – *false*

You would need to run a less powerful device for longer to get the same energy transfer as a more powerful device – *true*

C a power (W) $= \dfrac{100\,000\,(J)}{20\,(s)}$

         $= 5000\,W$

  b efficiency $= \dfrac{5000\,W}{20\,000\,W} \times 100$

         $= 25\%$

  c wasted power $= 20\,000\,W - 5000\,W$

         $= 15\,000\,W$

What you need to remember

rate
energy (J), time (s)
total, W, total, W
total, total

P1 Practice questions

01 type of energy store: thermal, elastic potential, kinetic, gravitational, chemical [1]
type of transfer pathway: conduction, electric current, radiation, forces [1]
02 elastic, force [2]
03 work done – the energy transferred when a force moves through a distance
power – the rate of energy transfer
efficiency – a ratio or percentage that tells you how good a device is at transferring energy
[all correct – 2, 1 correct – 1]
04.1 the amount of water [1]
04.2 efficiency

$= \dfrac{\text{useful energy transfer (J)}}{\text{total Input energy transfer (J)}} \times 100$ [1]

$= \dfrac{300\,000\,J}{400\,000\,J} \times 100$ [1]

$= 75\%$ [1]
04.3 less efficient [1]
04.4 cleaner / quicker [1]
04.5 conduction / radiation [1]
05.1 gravitational potential energy
= mass (kg) × gravitational field strength (N/kg) × change in height (m) [1]
= 50 kg × 10N/kg × 1.9 m [1]
= 950 J, which is about 1000 J [1]
05.2 $E_k = 0.5 \times$ mass $\times$ speed^2 [1]
= 0.5 × 50 kg × (6 m/s)^2 [1]
= 900 J [1]
05.3 to the thermal store of the surroundings [1]
05.4 elastic (potential) [1]

P2.1

A good conductors: copper, iron, aluminium;
good insulators: wool, glass, fibreglass
B rate, high
C Rod **X** has the highest thermal conductivity – *true*

Rod **Y** has the lowest thermal conductivity – *true*
Rod **Z** could be made of metal – *false*
The wax on the rods would melt more slowly if they had a larger diameter – *true*

What you need to remember

metals, non-metals
high
lower

P2.2

A the energy required to raise the temperature of 1 kg of a material by 1 °C
B **X, Y, Z**
C change in thermal energy (J) = mass (kg) × specific heat capacity (J/kg °C) × change in temperature (°C)
= 0.25 kg × 4200 J/ kg °C × 10 °C
= 10 500 J (11 000 J)
D it would take longer / twice as long

What you need to remember

1kg, 1
longer
energy, thermometer, mass

P2.3

A oil: stove, central heating system
coal or wood: stove, fire
gas: stove, central heating system, fire
B foam that is pumped into the gap between two walls
C building a house using thick bricks; putting layers of fibreglass in the loft; using aluminium foil behind the radiators
D 20

What you need to remember

oil, oil, wood
loft insulation, double glazing
two, cavity wall, thick / thicker, low / lower

P2 Practice questions

01 loft insulation – roof
thick bricks – walls
double glazing – windows
[all correct – 2, 2 correct – 1]
02 iron, steel, copper
[all correct – 2, 2 or 1 correct –1]
03.1 C [1]
03.2 infrared [1]
04.1 – *false*
04.2 – *true*
04.3 – *true*
04.4 – *true*
[all correct – 2, 2 or 1 correct –1]
05.1 a joulemeter [1]
     b thermometer [1]

05.2 specific heat capacity (J/kg °C)

$= \dfrac{45\,J}{1\,kg \times 20\,°C}$ [1]

$= 2.3\,(2.25)\,(J/kg\,°C)$ [1]

P3.1

A a coal, gas, nuclear
    b wind, solar, biofuel
    c coal, oil, gas
B living or recently living, methane, ethanol renewable, carbon-neutral
C In the core, radioactive material like uranium in the **nuclear fuel** rods – releases energy from each uranium **nucleus**, which heats a coolant. The coolant is pumped around a heat exchanger and – heats water to produce steam. The steam drives a **turbine**, which – drives a **generator** to produce electricity.
Uranium releases more energy per kilogram than – fossil fuels.

What you need to remember

coal, oil, gas
will
not
biofuels, methane, ethanol
nuclear, more

P3.2

A wind turbine – a generator on top of a tall tower
wave generator – a generator that floats on water
tidal barrage – a dam containing generators that traps water behind it
B Wind energy does not come from the Sun – *false*
Tidal power is more reliable than wave power – *true*
Wave power and tidal power both need moving water – *true*
There are no disadvantages to wind power – *false*
Wave generators can damage the habitats of wildlife – *true*
C water behind a dam high up falls through turbines and generators to generate electricity

What you need to remember

turbine
wave
turbines, hydroelectric
tidal
environment / habitats

P3.3

A a solar heating panel uses radiation from the Sun to heat water, and a solar cell panel generates electricity using radiation from the Sun
B Solar cells convert less than 10% of solar radiation into electricity – **D**

Solar panels only work on sunny days – **D**

You can generate electricity in remote places with solar cells – **A**

Solar cells are very expensive to buy – **D**

You do not need to be connected to a power station to use solar cells – **A**

Solar cells can be connected together to make solar cell panels – **N**

You need lots of solar cell panels to generate enough electricity to be useful – **D**

C   **Q, S, R, P, T**

What you need to remember

generate, heat
radioactive, water, steam, turbines

P3.4

A   Burning fossil fuels – produces carbon dioxide (a **greenhouse gas**), – which can be removed from the atmosphere with **carbon capture and storage**.

Burning fossil fuels – produces sulfur dioxide, – which must be removed from the atmosphere so it does not cause **acid rain**.

Using nuclear fuels – produces radioactive waste, – which needs to be stored safely for centuries.

B   Can cause noise pollution: *wind*

Can affect river estuaries and the habitats of plants and animals there – *tidal*

Depends on the weather to work – *wind, solar*

Involves large reservoirs of water, which can affect the habitats of plants and animals – *hydro*

Needs large areas to produce enough energy from these panels – *solar*

Not always available on demand – *wind, tidal, hydro, solar*

C   the energy from 1 kg of nuclear fuel is much bigger than the energy from 1 kg of a fossil fuel

What you need to remember

greenhouse, warming
radioactive
do not, remote, animals, plants

P3.5

A   global warming – carbon capture and storage

acid rain – remove sulfur from fuel

contamination from radioactive waste – find a secure place to store waste

B   increasing, expensive, decommission, expensive, cheap, range of resources

C   a   i   0–8 / midnight–8 am
        ii   8–24 / 8 am–midnight
    b   by pumping water up into a reservoir at a hydroelectric power station

What you need to remember

coal, pumped, expensive, decommission
carbon capture, cheap, expensive

P3 Practice questions

01.1   coal, uranium, oil, gas [all correct – 2,
                                    1–3 correct – 1]

01.2   coal, oil, gas [1 for all three]

02   **B** before **D**, [1] **D** before **E**, [1] **E** before **A**, [1] **A** before **C** [1]

03.1   solar heating panel [1]

03.2   solar cell [1]

03.3   small [1]

03.4   is not, are [2]

04   Hydroelectric power involves pumping water – into a lake, then letting the water fall down – and the water turns a turbine and generator. [1]

Geothermal power involves pumping water – into the ground where hot rocks turn it to steam – and the steam turns a turbine and generator. [1]

05.1   total percentage
       = percentage for oil + coal + gas [1]
       = 1% + 31% + 46% [1]
       = 78% [1]

05.2   one from: causes acid rain, produces greenhouse gases, produces more global warming [1]

05.3   one from: wind, waves, tidal, geothermal, hydroelectric, solar [1]

05.4   appropriate advantage, e.g., does not produce greenhouse gases, cheap to run [1]

appropriate disadvantage, e.g., expensive to install, unreliable [1]

06   **Sasha's reply:** I don't think we should because they produce radioactive waste [1] and they are expensive to decommission. [1]

Dev's reply: I don't think we should because they are expensive to install [1] and they can harm wildlife. [1]

P4.1

A   first column, top to bottom: bulb / lamp, ammeter, diode, cell

second column, top to bottom: resistor, variable resistor, fuse, battery (of cells)

B   A current is a flow of **electrons** – *true*

Charge is measured in amperes – *false*

Conventional current flows from the negative to the positive terminal of a battery – *false*

The current before a component is bigger than the current after a component – *false*

Current is the charge in coulombs flowing per second – *true*

Current gets smaller further away from the battery – *false*

C   2 min = 120 s

$$\text{current} = \frac{12\,C}{120\,s}$$

$$= 0.1\,A$$

What you need to remember

symbol
cells
rate

$$(A),\ \frac{\text{charge (C)}}{\text{time (s)}}$$

P4.2

A   **W, Y**

B   directly proportional, temperature, reverses direction

C   potential difference $= \dfrac{240\,J}{20\,C}$

$$= 12\,V$$

D   resistance $= \dfrac{12\,V}{2\,A}$

$$= 6\,\Omega$$

What you need to remember

energy, energy
(V), energy (J), charge (C),
(Ω), potential difference (V), current (A)
directly proportional, reverse

P4.3

A   ammeter

B   lamp; diode; (fixed) resistor

C   light-dependent resistor: dark, light
    thermistor: cold, hot

D   diode
    a diode only lets the current flow in one direction

What you need to remember

increases
low, high, forward
decreases, decreases

P4.4

A   a   **Y** – 0.2
        Z – 0.2
    b   the current everywhere in a series circuit is the same

B   a   3 V
    b   6 V
    c   the potential differences across the components in a series circuit add up to the potential difference across the cell

C   smaller, bigger
    double
    double

What you need to remember

current, potential difference, adding
add
increases, less

P4.5

A   a   **Y** – 0.2
        Z – 0.4

b the current at **Y** will be the same as the current at **X** because the bulbs are identical and the p.d. across them is the same; the current at **Z** is the sum of the currents at **X** and **Y**

B **a** 3 V
b 3 V
c the potential differences across the components in a parallel circuit are equal to the potential difference across the cell

C double
bigger, smaller
half

What you need to remember

potential difference, current, currents, smaller
(A), p.d. (V), resistance (Ω)
decreases, increases

P4 Practice questions

01 potential difference – the energy transferred to or by a charge
current – the rate of flow of charge
resistance – how easy or hard it is for charge to flow through a component
[all correct – 2, one correct – 1]

02.1 cell [1]
02.2 variable resistor [1]
02.3 **C** is a diode, but **D** is a light-emitting diode. [1]
02.4 thermistor [1]
03.1 parallel; [1] you can operate the bulbs independently [1]
03.2 both lamps will go off; [1] the circuit is wired with both bulbs in series [1]
03.3 10 Ω + 10 Ω = 20 Ω [1]
03.4 smaller, more, the same [3]
04.1 current (A) = $\dfrac{\text{charge (C)}}{\text{time (s)}}$ [1]

$= \dfrac{20\,\text{C}}{40\,\text{s}}$

$= 0.5\,\text{A}$ [1]

04.2 the current is proportional to the p.d. [1] as long as the temperature remains constant [1]

04.3 resistance (Ω) = $\dfrac{\text{p.d. (V)}}{\text{current (A)}}$ [1]

$= \dfrac{12\,\text{V}}{0.5\,\text{A}}$

$= 24\,\Omega$ [1]

04.4 the direction of motion of the turntable would reverse [1]

P5.1

A The mains supplies – alternating current, – which flows backwards and forwards.
A battery supplies – direct current, – which flows only in one direction.

B p.d. from zero to the peak
time for one cycle, 1 ÷ time period
live, neutral
Grid

C frequency (Hz) = $\dfrac{1}{0.2\,\text{s}}$

$= 5\,\text{Hz}$

What you need to remember

one, reverses
−230 V, +230 V, zero / 0
network
maximum, zero, time (for one cycle)
Hz, time period (s)

P5.2

A earth: green/yellow; live: brown; neutral: blue

B The plug casing is made of – hard plastic because – it need to be a rigid insulator.
Each wire is made of – copper because – it needs to conduct electricity.
The insulation on the wire is made of – soft plastic because – it needs to be an insulator that is flexible.

C metal, longest, live, cannot

What you need to remember

plastic, insulator
copper, insulating
brown, blue, green, yellow
longest / centre, casing

P5.3

A Y
B 15 kW = 15 000 W
1 hour = 3600 s
energy transferred = 15 000 W × 3600 s
= 54 000 000 J

C power = 230 V × 1.5 A
= 345 W (350 W)

D **a** current = $\dfrac{1000\,\text{W}}{230\,\text{V}}$

$= 4.35\,\text{A}\ (= 4.4\,\text{A})$

b 5 A

What you need to remember

energy (J), power (W), time (s)
(W), potential difference (V), current (A)
(A), power (W), potential difference (V)

P5.4

A The electrons transfer energy to the resistor and heat it up.
B 4 mA = 0.004 A
charge = 0.004 A × 0.1 s
= 0.0004 C
C energy, more, 6 J
D energy transferred = 300 000 C × 230 V
= 69 000 000 J

What you need to remember

(C), current (A), time (s)
heat up
(J), potential difference (V), charge (C)
energy, energy

P5.5

A **a** potential difference, current
b time

B power = 230 V × 15 A
= 3450 W
= 3500 W to 2 significant figures

C 30 minutes = 1800 s
energy transferred = 2000 W × 1800 s
= 3 600 000 J

D 70% efficient = 0.7 as a decimal fraction
4000 kJ = 4 000 000 J
useful energy = 0.7 × 4 000 000 J
= 2 800 000 J

What you need to remember

energy (J), power (W), time (s) (J), efficiency,
energy supplied (J)

P5 Practice questions

01 earth: green/yellow; [1] neutral: blue; [1] live: brown [1]
02.1 **A** [1]
02.2 **C** [1]
02.3 **B** [1]
02.4 **B** and **C** [1]
02.5 National Grid [1]
03.1 hard plastic [1]
03.2 it is rigid/won't bend/it is an insulator [1]
03.3 soft plastic [1]
03.4 it can bend/is flexible/it is an insulator [1]

04 current = $\dfrac{\text{power}}{\text{potential difference}}$ [1]

$= \dfrac{1100\,\text{W}}{230\,\text{V}}$ [1]

$= 4.78\,\text{A}\ (= 4.8\,\text{A})$ [1]

so she needs a 5 A fuse [1]

05.1 2 min = 120 s
energy transferred = power × time [1]
= 800 W × 120 s [1]
= 96 000 J [1]

05.2 as the electrons move through the wire they collide with the ions/atoms, [1] which vibrate more [1]

05.3 time = 6 min = 360 s
charge = current × time [1]
= 5.2 A × 360 s [1]
= 1872 C = 1900 C [1]

05.4 time = 24 × 60 × 60 = 86 400 [1]
energy transferred = power × time
= 420 W × 86 400 s [1]
= 36 288 000 J = 36 000 000 J [1]

P6.1

A density = $\dfrac{70\,\text{kg}}{0.07\,\text{m}^3}$

$= 1000\,\text{kg/m}^3$

B To find the density of a regular solid, such as a brick, – you use a digital balance to find the mass – and measure the volume with a ruler.

To find the density of a liquid, such as water, – you measure the mass of an empty and full measuring cylinder – and measure the volume with a measuring cylinder.
To find the density of an irregular solid, such as a stone, – you use a digital balance to find the mass – and measure the volume of water it displaces.

C An object floats if its density is less than that of water.

What you need to remember

mass, volume, kg/m³
mass (kg), volume (m³)
density, volume, mass, density
mass, volume
smaller than

P6.2

A solid – Particles are held next to each other in fixed positions.
liquid – Particles move at random and are in contact with each other.
gas – Particles move about randomly and are far apart.

B A solid – melts to form – a liquid.
A solid – sublimates to form – a solid.
A liquid – vaporises or boils to form – a gas.
A liquid – solidifies or freezes to form – a solid.
A gas – condenses to form – a liquid.
A gas – sublimates to form – a solid.

C most, least
does not, does not
are not

What you need to remember

gas, liquid, solid
solid, gas
mass

P6.3

A dotted line: melting point
first curved section: solid
horizontal section: solid + liquid
second curved section: liquid

B horizontal, freezing point, latent heat

C This process happens at the boiling point of the liquid – *boiling*
The mass does not change – *boiling, evaporation*
The particles escape only from the surface of the liquid – *boiling, evaporation*
This process happens at or below the boiling point of the liquid – *evaporation*

What you need to remember

melts, freezes, boils, condenses
horizontal
Boiling, vaporisation

P6.4

A the kinetic energy of particles in a gas; the energy of vibration of the particles in a solid;

the gravitational potential energy of the particles in a liquid

B If you heat a substance – its internal energy increases.
If you heat a substance and its temperature changes – the kinetic energy of the particles increases.
If you heat a substance and its temperature does not change – the potential energy of the particles increases.

C more, stronger, more

D particles repeatedly collide with the surface of the container

What you need to remember

increases
attraction
kinetic, potential
colliding

P6.5

A measured in joules – *latent heat*
energy to change the state of 1 kg of a substance – *specific latent heat*
measured in J/kg – *specific latent heat*
energy to change the state of a substance – *latent heat*

B R, Q, P, S

C 334 kJ/kg = 334 000 J/kg
thermal energy for melting ice = 334 000 J/kg × 0.03 kg = 10 020 J

What you need to remember

energy, temperature
1 kg, temperature
(J), mass (kg), specific latent heat (J/kg)
melt, boil

P6.6

A . . . the average speed of the gas molecules increases – *true*
. . . the molecules get hotter – *false*
. . . the molecules get bigger – *false*
. . . the molecules collide more often with the surface that encloses the gas – *true*

B increases, more, more

C Brownian motion / observing smoke particles that you can see being moved by air molecules that you cannot see

What you need to remember

pressure
increases, more, increases
random

P6 Practice questions

01 kg/m³ [1]
02.1 melting [1]
02.2 condensing [1]
02.3 subliming [1]
03.1 collide, force [2]
03.2 increase, more, more [3]
04.1 70 °C [1]

04.2 the particles are close together but begin to move faster [3]

05.1 B [1]

05.2 density = $\dfrac{\text{mass}}{\text{volume}}$ [1]

$= \dfrac{2000 \text{ kg}}{0.5 \text{ m}^3}$ [1]

$= 4000 \text{ kg/m}^3$ [1]

06 D before B, [1] B before C, [1] C before A, [1] A before E, [1]

07 mass = 2 g = 0.002 kg
thermal energy for a change of state
= 0.002 kg × 334 000 J/kg
= 668 J
temperature change = 20 °C
change in thermal energy
= 0.002 kg × 4200 J/kg °C × 20 °C
= 168 J
total energy = 668 J + 168 J
= 836 J = 840 J [4]

P7.1

A alpha, beta, gamma

B Radioactivity is the name of the property of materials that emit radiation – *correct*
The particles or waves that stable nuclei emit are called radiation – *correct*
If something is random, you can predict when it will happen – *incorrect*
A nucleus that emits radiation is unstable – *correct*
A nucleus that does not emit radiation is random – *incorrect*

corrected versions:
If something is random, you cannot predict when it will happen
A nucleus that does not emit radiation is stable.

C **alpha radiation** – paper – α
beta radiation – aluminium – β
gamma radiation – lead – γ

What you need to remember

unstable, stable
alpha, beta, gamma
random

P7.2

A alpha, metal, went through, came back, in the middle, positively

B If the 'plum pudding' model were correct – either all the particles would go through, or all of them would come back.
Models are rejected if – they do not explain experimental observations.
The 'plum pudding' model could not explain why – some particles were scattered through large angles.

What you need to remember

alpha, large
plum pudding
massive / small, positively

P7.3

A a $^{14}_{6}C$ $^{12}_{6}C$

b the same number of protons but a different number of neutrons

B In alpha decay a nucleus loses two protons and two neutrons.
In beta decay a neutron changes into a proton and an electron.

C a Y
b X

What you need to remember

same, different, same, different
two / 2, two / 2, four / 4, two / 2
neutron, proton, electron, does not change, one / 1

P7.4

A top label: α radiation
middle label: β radiation
bottom label: γ radiation

B Alpha radiation – has a range of a few cm in air, – consists of two protons and two neutrons, – and is the most ionising.
Beta radiation – has a range of about 1 m in air, – consists of a fast-moving electron, – and is moderately ionising.
Gamma radiation – has an infinite range in air, – consists of electromagnetic radiation, – and is the least ionising.

C it ionises atoms / molecules. This can damage cells / kill cells / cause cancer / mutations.

What you need to remember

paper, aluminium, lead
a few cm, about 1m, infinite
two / 2, two / 2, fast, electromagnetic
most, least
ionise, damage

P7.5

A count rate – the number of counts per second on a Geiger counter
activity – the number of decays per second
becquerel – the unit of activity

B Half-life is the time for the number of unstable nuclei to halve.
Half-life is the time for the activity to halve.

C 45, the same, equal to

What you need to remember

halve
decreases
halve

P7 Practice questions

01 is stopped by paper – *alpha* [1]
has the symbol β – *beta* [1]
travels only a few centimetres in air – *alpha* [1]
is stopped only by lead and concrete – *gamma* [1]
has the symbol γ – *gamma* [1]
travels only about 1 m in air – *beta* [1]

02.1 alpha [1]
02.2 beta or gamma [1]
02.3 beta [1]
03.1 **B** [1]
03.2 **A** [1]
03.3 **C** [1]
04 most of the alpha particles went through, but some were scattered back/ through large angles [2]
05 **C, D** [2]
06.1 ionising radiation can damage or kill cells [1]
06.2 $^{101}_{43}Tc \rightarrow {}^{101}_{44}Ru + {}^{0}_{-1}\beta$ [2]

P8.1

A has magnitude – *scalar, vector*
has direction – *vector*
can be represented by an arrow – *vector*

B force, velocity, acceleration

C Y

D arrow starting from head of hammer, pointing left

What you need to remember

distance
magnitude, direction, magnitude
direction, magnitude

P8.2

A A force can change the shape of an object, for example, – a tennis ball hitting the ground.
A force can change the motion of an object, for example, – accelerating on a bicycle.
A force can start an object moving that was at rest, for example, – a rocket taking off.

B friction – *contact*
electrostatic – *non-contact*
gravity – *non-contact*
air resistance – *contact*
tension – *contact*
magnetic – *non-contact*

C equal, gravitational, the same size friction, friction

What you need to remember

shape, motion, stationary, newtons
contact
equal, opposite

P8.3

A the single force that you can use to replace all the forces acting on an object

B If there is no resultant force on a stationary object it will not move – *true*
If there is a resultant force on an object that is moving with a steady speed it will always speed up – *false*
If there is a resultant force on an object that is not moving, then it will move with a steady speed – *false*
If there is no resultant force on an object that is moving with a steady speed, then it will slow down – *false*
If there is a resultant force on an object that is moving with a steady speed, then it may change direction – *true*

C 7, 3, **4, to the left**
10, 20, **10, to the right**
80, 150, **70, to the right**

What you need to remember

same
zero
greater, zero
add, difference

P8.4

A Y

B circle with dot in the centre, rectangle with dot in the centre, triangle with dot in the centre

C below, cross

What you need to remember

point
centre
below
line

P8 Practice questions

01 30 m north; [1] 2 m/s south [1]

02 friction, tension, air resistance [all correct – 2, 2 or 1 correct – 1]

03.1 change the shape of an object or start a stationary object moving [1]

03.2 → 3N; [1] 0N; [1] ← 1N [1]

04.1 Earth, chair [2]

04.2 the same as [1]

04.3 the same size as [1]

05 not moving, 1 N to the right, **accelerate** [1]
moving at 3 m/s to the left, none, **move at 3 m/s to the left** [1]
moving at 3 m/s to the left, 2 N to the right, **slow down** [1]
not moving, none, **not move** [1]

06.1 total distance = 10 cm + 5 cm + 8 cm + 5 cm
= 28 cm [1]

06.2 displacement up/down
= 10 cm up – 8 cm down
= 2 cm up [1]
displacement right/left = 5 cm right – 5 cm left
= 0 cm [1]
so final displacement = 2 cm up [1]

07.1
- Attach a string to the suspension point with a mass on the end so the string is in front of the card.
- Draw a line on the card where the string is.
- Repeat from a different suspension point.
- Where the lines cross is the centre of mass. [4]

07.2 it is below the suspension point [1]

P9.1

A Y

B If the line on the graph is horizontal – the object is stationary.
If the line on the graph is straight and steep – the object is travelling at high speed.
If the line on the graph is straight and not very steep – the object is travelling at low speed.

C $speed = \dfrac{10\ m}{2.5}$
$= 4\ m/s$

D a distance travelled = 5 m/s × 10 s
$= 50\ m$

b $time = \dfrac{200\ m}{5\ m/s}$
$= 40\ s$

What you need to remember

m/s, distance (m), time (s),
stationary, steady speed
gradient

P9.2

A This has direction – *vector*
This has magnitude – *scalar, vector*

B 10 m/s north, 38 mph south

C change in velocity = 5 m/s – 2 m/s
$= 3\ m/s$

$acceleration = \dfrac{3\ m/s}{10\ s}$
$= 0.3\ m/s^2$

D 0, 20 – *accelerating*
8, 20 – *decelerating*
4, 2 – *decelerating*

What you need to remember

direction
vector, scalar
(m/s²), change in velocity (m/s), time (s)
slows down

P9.3

A connect a motion sensor to a computer, and point the motion sensor at the moving object

B positive, speeding up, negative, slowing down, is not

C 12, 4, 10, 0.8

What you need to remember

motion sensor
gradient, zero
gradient, negative

P9.4

A The speed in the first 10 s – is 2 m/s.
The speed in the second 10 s – is zero.
The speed at any time in the last 10 s – is the gradient of the graph at that time.

B The magnitude of the acceleration is the same as the magnitude of the deceleration.
The train travels at a steady speed for 30 minutes.

What you need to remember

gradient
gradient

P9 Practice questions

01 $speed = \dfrac{1\ m}{2.5\ s}$ [1]

02 A vector has magnitude and direction, but a scalar has magnitude only. [1]

03 **1**, 5, 5 [1]
10, **20**, 2 [1]
100, 300, **3** [1]

04 $acceleration = \dfrac{change\ in\ speed}{time}$ [1]
$= \dfrac{0.5\ m/s}{0.05\ s}$ [1]
$= 10\ m/s^2$ [1]

05.1 between 1000 m and 3000 m [1]
05.2 between 30 minutes and 40 minutes [1]
05.3 because displacement is distance from a particular point [1]

06.1 constant positive [1] acceleration [1]
06.2 travelling at a steady speed [1]
06.3 decelerating/slowing down, with a constant negative [1] acceleration [1]

07.1 $acceleration = \dfrac{change\ in\ speed}{time}$
$= \dfrac{7\ m/s}{10\ s}$ [1]
$= 0.7\ m/s^2$ [1]

07.2 zero [1]
08.1 half [1]
08.2 The speed changes by the same amount (7 m/s) [1] but takes twice the time. [1]

P10.1

A increases, stays the same, **increases**
decreases, stays the same, **decreases**
stays the same, increases, **decreases**
stays the same, decreases, **increases**

B proportional, doubles, stays the same inversely proportional, halves, stays the same

C mass = 100 g = 0.1 kg
resultant force = 0.1 kg × 3 m/s²
= 0.3 N

What you need to remember

increase, mass
smaller
(N), mass (kg), acceleration (m/s²)
rest, constant/steady

P10.2

A 10

B Mass is the quantity of matter in an object. Weight is the force of gravity acting on an object.

C 1, 9.8, **98**
3, 9.8, 29
10, 1.6, **16**

D Y, W, Z, X

What you need to remember

force, matter
10
terminal frictional, zero

P10.3

A Braking distance is – the distance that the car travels when the brakes are on.
Thinking distance is – the distance that the car travels while the driver reacts.
Stopping distance is – the thinking distance plus the braking distance.

B snow / ice on the road: no, yes
being tired: yes, no
speed: yes, yes
drinking alcohol: yes, no
using a phone: yes, no

C force = 1000 kg × 4 m/s²
= 4000 N = 4 kN

What you need to remember

driving
thinking, braking
braking, thinking
(N), mass (kg), acceleration (m/s²)

P10.5

A Z

B extension = 4.5 cm – 3 cm = 1.5 cm = 0.015 m
force = 40 N/m × 0.015 m
= 0.48 N

C 5, straight, directly proportional
non-linear, curve

What you need to remember

elastic
difference
directly proportional, elasticity, linear
elasticity, non-linear, proportional

P10 Practice questions

01 force, mass [2]

02 If the force on a trolley increases – and the mass stays the same, – the acceleration increases.
    If the mass of a trolley increases – and the force stays the same – the acceleration decreases.
    If you double the force – and you double the mass, – the acceleration stays the same.
                    [all correct – 2, one correct – 1]

03.1 one from: road conditions, conditions of brakes, speed [1]

03.2 one from: drinking alcohol, drug taking, tiredness, being distracted [1]

04 1, 2, **2** [1]
    0.5, 2, **1** [1]
    100, 0.02, **2** [1]

05.1 subtract [1]
05.2 divide [1]
05.3 5 N [1]
05.4 two appropriate measurements used (e.g. 2 N/2 cm, 4 N/4 cm) [1]

$$\text{spring constant} = \frac{\text{force}}{\text{extension}} \text{ [1]}$$
$$= \frac{4 \text{ N}}{0.04 \text{ m}} \text{ [1]}$$
$$= 100 \text{ N/m [1]}$$

06.1 force of the air on the ball/air resistance [1]
06.2 3 m/s [1]
06.3 the ball accelerates [1] because the forces on the ball are unbalanced; [1] the weight is bigger than the air resistance [1]
06.4 the ball travels at a steady speed / terminal velocity [1]
      because the forces on the ball are balanced / the resultant force is zero [1] and the air resistance is equal to the weight [1]

P11.1

A energy, information
B Oscillations are in the same direction as the energy transfer – *longitudinal*
   Oscillations are perpendicular to the direction of energy transfer – *transverse*
   Sound waves are an example – *longitudinal*
   Electromagnetic waves are an example – *transverse*
C a mechanical, compressions, rarefactions
   a mechanical
   electromagnetic
   can, cannot

What you need to remember

information
transverse, ripples, electromagnetic
longitudinal, sound
medium

P11.2

A The distance from one peak to the next peak is the wavelength – *correct*

Frequency is the number of waves per second – *correct*
The unit of frequency is seconds – *incorrect*
The unit of wavelength is metres – *correct*
The distance from a peak to a trough is the amplitude – *incorrect*

corrected versions:
The unit of frequency is hertz.
The distance from the centre (equilibrium) of a wave to the peak or trough is the amplitude.

B a $\text{period (s)} = \frac{1}{200} \text{ Hz}$
         $= 0.005 \text{ s}$
   b $\text{speed} = 660 \text{ Hz} \times 0.5 \text{ m}$
         $= 330 \text{ m/s}$

What you need to remember

maximum, peak, trough
same, crest / peak
(s), frequency (Hz)
(m/s), frequency (Hz), wavelength (m)

P11.4

A R
B W, X, V, Y, Z
C total distance travelled by the sound
   $= 2 \times$ distance to wall
   $= 2 \times 150 \text{ m}$
   $= 300 \text{ m}$
   $\text{speed} = \frac{300 \text{ m}}{0.9 \text{ s}}$
         $= 333.3 \text{ m/s}$
         $= 330 \text{ m/s}$

What you need to remember

reflects
time, distance

$(\text{m/s}), \dfrac{\text{distance (m)}}{\text{time (s)}}$

P11 Practice questions

01 The period of the wave is the time for one whole wave. [1]
    The frequency is the number of waves per second. [1]

02 wavelength: **D** or **F**
    amplitude: **A** or **C**
                    [4 – 1 for each correct letter]

03 A mechanical wave – does need a medium to travel through, – such as sound.
    An electromagnetic wave – does not need a medium to travel through, – such as light.
                    [2 – 1 for each correct pair of lines]

04.1 in the same direction as [1]
04.2 perpendicular to [1]
04.3 compressions, rarefactions [2]
05.1 speed = frequency × wavelength [1]
      = 1000 Hz × 1.5 m [1]
      = 1500 m/s [1]

05.2 $\text{period} = \dfrac{1}{\text{frequency}}$ [1]
      $= \dfrac{1}{1000 \text{ Hz}}$ [1]
      = 0.001 s [1]

06.1 stopwatch / stopclock [1], measuring tape / metre ruler / trundle wheel [1]
06.2 they started the timer when they saw the sound being made [1] and stopped the timer when they heard the echo [1]
06.3 total distance travelled by the sound
      $= 2 \times$ distance to wall
      $= 2 \times 200 \text{ m}$
      $= 400 \text{ m}$ [1]
      $\text{speed} = \dfrac{400 \text{ m}}{1.3 \text{ s}}$ [1]
      $= 307.7 \text{ m/s}$ [1]
      $= 310 \text{ m/s}$ [1]
06.4 repeat the experiment/take more measurements of time and calculate the mean time [1]

P12.1

A a *radio*, microwaves, infrared, *visible*, ultraviolet, X-rays, *gamma*
   b blue: radio
   c red: gamma
   d green outline: gamma
   e yellow outline: visible
B electromagnetic waves transfer energy from a source to a detector
C a blue: 350 nm
   b red: 700 nm
D wavelength = 3 cm = 0.03 m
   speed = 10 000 000 000 Hz × 0.03 m
         = 300 000 000 m/s

What you need to remember

microwave, infrared, visible light, ultraviolet, X-rays
biggest, smallest, smallest, biggest
visible, 350 nm, 700 nm
source, detector
speed (m/s), frequency (Hz), wavelength (m)

P12.2

A prism, spectrum, image, digital
B infrared scanner in medicine: detects infrared
   remote control: emits infrared, transfers information
   infrared camera: detects infrared
   electric heater: emits infrared
C Y
D We use microwaves for satellite TV – because they can pass through the atmosphere.
   Microwaves and radio waves can be hazardous – because they heat up parts of the body.
   We use radio waves for connecting computers to other devices – because they transmit information without wires.

What you need to remember

waves
information, optical
radio, microwaves, microwaves, radio waves
radio, microwaves, infrared

P12.3

A X, Z, W, Y
B S
C long, bigger, less, less
   more, shorter, reflected

What you need to remember

distance, spread, information
microwaves
evidence
visible, infrared

P12.4

A Ultraviolet waves lie between X-rays and
   gamma rays in the electromagnetic
   spectrum – *false*
   Ultraviolet waves can cause lung
   cancer – *false*
   Ultraviolet waves can cause skin cancer – *true*
   Ultraviolet waves have a longer wavelength
   than visible light – *false*
B X, Z
C R, P, S, Q, T

What you need to remember

shorter, skin
hospitals/medicine
bacteria, sterilise, cancer
ionising
damage

P12.5

A producing images of broken limbs – *X-rays*
   killing cancer cells inside the body –
   gamma rays
   killing skin cancer cells – *X-rays*
B R, S, P, Q, U, T
C X-rays are ionising radiation, which can
   damage (the DNA of) cells, and cause cancer
D circle: thick metal
   box: skin

What you need to remember

cancer
ionising
absorb

P12 Practice questions

01.1 C [1]
01.2 F [1]

01.3 radio waves (**B**), microwaves (**D**), infrared
      radiation (**A**), visible light (**F**), ultraviolet
      radiation (**G**), X-rays (**E**), gamma rays (**C**)
      B before **D**, [1] **D** before **A**, [1] **A** before **F**,
      [1] **F** before **G**, [1] **G** before **E**, [1]
      E before **C** [1]
02.1 visible / infrared [1]
02.2

      [light reflected from the inside – 1, at
      equal (large) angles – 1]

03   A mobile phone – emits and absorbs –
      radio waves / microwaves. [1]
      A TV aerial – emits and absorbs –
      radio waves. [1]
      A remote control – emits – infrared
      radiation. [1]
      Photographic film – absorbs – visible light. [1]
04   short, atmosphere, spread [3]
05.1 X-rays [1]
05.2 the X-rays are absorbed by bone; [1] they
      do not reach the CCD / photographic
      film, so no radiation = white; [1] the
      X-rays reach the CCD / photographic
      film, so radiation = black [1]
05.3 radiation that removes electrons from
      atoms / molecules when it passes
      through matter [1]
05.4 gamma/ultraviolet [1]
05.5 one from: shielding, reducing time
      spent near source, increasing distance
      between source and person [1]
06   wavelength $= \dfrac{\text{speed}}{\text{frequency}}$ [1]

      $= \dfrac{300\ 000\ 000 \text{ m/s}}{100\ 000\ 000 \text{ Hz}}$ [1]

      $= 3$ m [1]

P13.1

A north, …brought together with…, north, *repel*
   north, …brought together with…, south,
   attract
   south, …brought together with…, north,
   attract
   south, …brought together with…, south, *repel*
B arrows on three lines coming out to left,
   pointing left; arrows on three lines coming out
   to right, pointing left; arrows on lines above
   and beneath the magnet, pointing right
C If you put a piece of magnetic material in a
   magnetic field, – it will become an induced
   magnet.
   If you put iron in a magnetic field, – it will
   become magnetic but will lose its magnetism
   easily.
   If you put steel in a magnetic field, – it will
   become magnetic and will not lose its
   magnetism easily.

What you need to remember

repel, attract
north, south
induced
steel
iron

P13.2

A concentric circles getting further apart;
   arrows to show field is clockwise
B Parallel magnetic field lines show that – the
   field is uniform, – such as in the middle of a
   solenoid.
   Magnetic field lines that are getting closer
   together show that – the magnetic field is
   getting stronger, – such as near the end of a
   solenoid.
   The direction of the arrow on the field line
   shows – the direction of the field – or the
   force on a magnetic material.
C reverse, same
   far apart, close together

What you need to remember

circles
parallel
increasing, reverse
parallel

P13 Practice questions

01 bar magnet, wire with an electric current
    flowing in it [2]
02 like poles repel, unlike poles attract [2]
03 The magnetic field inside a solenoid is
    uniform. [1]
    The magnetic field around a solenoid has the
    same shape as that around a bar magnet [1]
04.1 opposite, opposite [2]
04.2 decreases, increases [2]
04.3 larger, closer together [2]
05.1 induced [1]
05.2 iron, steel [2]
06.1 B, A, C, D [2]
06.2 solenoid **B** has an iron core, but solenoid
      A has an air core; [1] when the iron core
      is in the magnetic field of the wire it
      becomes an induced magnet, [1] which
      means the magnetic field of the solenoid
      is equal to that of the coil + that of the
      iron, so the solenoid is stronger [1]
06.3 the compass needle is always in the
      same direction, [1]
      because the field is uniform [1]

Appendix 1: Physics equations

You should be able to remember and apply the following equations, using SI units, for your assessments.

Word equation	Symbol equation
weight = mass × gravitational field strength	$W = mg$
force applied to a spring = spring constant × extension	$F = ke$
acceleration = $\dfrac{\text{change in velocity}}{\text{time taken}}$	$a = \dfrac{\Delta v}{t}$
gravitational potential energy = mass × gravitational field strength × height	$E_p = mgh$
power = $\dfrac{\text{work done}}{\text{time}}$	$P = \dfrac{W}{t}$
efficiency = useful power output ÷ total power input	
charge flow = current × time	$Q = It$
power = potential difference × current	$P = VI$
energy transferred = power × time	$E = Pt$
density = $\dfrac{\text{mass}}{\text{volume}}$	$\rho = \dfrac{m}{V}$
work done = force × distance (along the line of action of the force)	$W = Fs$
distance travelled = speed × time	$s = vt$
resultant force = mass × acceleration	$F = ma$
kinetic energy = 0.5 × mass × (speed)²	$E_k = \dfrac{1}{2}mv^2$
power = $\dfrac{\text{energy transferred}}{\text{time}}$	$P = \dfrac{E}{t}$
efficiency = $\dfrac{\text{useful output energy transfer}}{\text{total input energy transfer}}$	
wave speed = frequency × wavelength	$v = f\lambda$
potential difference = current × resistance	$V = IR$
power = current² × resistance	$P = I^2R$
energy transferred = charge flow × potential difference	$E = QV$

You should be able to select and apply the following equations from the Physics equation sheet.

Word equation	Symbol equation
(final velocity)² – (initial velocity)² = 2 × acceleration × distance	$v^2 - u^2 = 2as$
elastic potential energy = 0.5 × spring constant × extension²	$E_e = \dfrac{1}{2}ke^2$
period = $\dfrac{1}{\text{frequency}}$	
change in thermal energy = mass × specific heat capacity × temperature change	$\Delta E = mc\Delta\theta$
thermal energy for a change of state = mass × specific latent heat	$E = mL$